W9-CHN-323

small
gardens

small
gardens

DAVID SQUIRE

p

This is a Parragon Publishing Book
This edition published in 2004

Parragon Publishing
Queen Street House
4 Queen Street
Bath BA1 1HE, UK

Copyright © Parragon 2002

All rights reserved. No part of this publication may be reproduced, stored
in a retrieval system or transmitted, in any form or by any means, electronic, mechanical,
photocopying, recording or otherwise, without the prior
permission of the copyright holder.

Created and produced by The Bridgewater Book Company Ltd.

ISBN: 1-40543-965-3

Printed in China

NOTE
For growing and harvesting, calendar information applies
only to the Northern Hemisphere (US zones 5–9).

contents

introduction

Few gardens are large and nowadays most are less than the size of a tennis court. But whatever the size it is possible to grow plants in an imaginative way that creates an outdoor area for family living. Climbers on free-standing trellises are superb for providing privacy and spectacular displays of flowers and leaves, while plants in window boxes and hanging baskets decorate walls and windows; those in tubs and planters create color at patio level. Many small gardens do not have a lawn and this clearly eliminates the need to buy, house,

and maintain a mower. However, an ornamental lawn-type feature can be created from chamomile and a decorative path from thyme. Both do not have the hard wearing nature of grass, but in a small area produce exciting features that are sure to capture attention.

Inspirational yet practical

This all-color book is packed with practical information about improving both an existing garden and a brand new one, perhaps surrounded by a sea of rubble left by the builders of the new

house. Assessing and improving soil is described, as well as gardening on slopes and dealing with varying amounts of light and shade. A wide range of paths for small gardens, as well as walls, fences, and steps, is described so that the right one can be selected. And, of course, a firm-surfaced patio, terrace, or courtyard is essential; much of the pleasure derived from a garden is to use it as an outdoor living area. Pergolas, arches, trellises, arbours, flowering tunnels, and porches are other important features and their range and use are thoroughly detailed. All gardeners have a preference for specific garden features and these range from lawns that enable children and animals to play safely, to water gardens, thyme paths, rock gardens, groups of fragrant plants, and, of course, a vast range of roses from bush types to ramblers and climbers. These are all covered, with advice on how to integrate them into a garden.

▲ *Whether in sunlight or shade a border can become awash with colorful flowers and attractive leaves. There are plants for all places.*

HEIGHTS AND SPREADS

The heights and spreads given for shrubs and trees refer to 15–20-year-old specimens growing in good conditions. Eventually, these plants may grow even larger.

Using plants in a garden

In a small garden it is essential to plan the positions of plants so that they give the best possible display. Color-themed gardens, perhaps dominant in pink-and-red, blue-and-purple, yellow-and-gold, and white-and-silver are popular, while those with variegated foliage remain attractive over a long period. More frequently, plants are grown in mixed-color borders, where flowers of all hues and shapes jostle side by side to form a traditional English flower border. To create an even more impressive display from single-color themes, position them against color-enhancing backgrounds provided by hedges, such as yew and other conifers. Window boxes and hanging baskets can also be given this added design quality by positioning them against color-washed walls. Growing your own food is important and fresh salad plants are possible in even the smallest garden. Tomatoes and lettuces grow well in growing-bags, while herbs are ideal for planting in ornamental pots and planters. There are even planters with cup-like holes in their sides that enable a wide range of small herbs to be grown in a confined area. Additionally, containers help to restrain the invasive nature of mints that after a few years often become a nuisance in a herb border. Dwarf rootstocks now enable apples to be grown in large tubs on a patio, while both apples and pears can be grown as espaliers or cordons near to a wall or in a narrow bed perhaps alongside a path. Peaches, nectarines, and plums can be grown in fan-shaped forms against walls and strong fences that are sheltered and in full sun.

▲ *Achillea is an ideal herbaceous perennial for growing in a dry, sunny border. Its flowers are ideal for cutting and displaying indoors.*

▼ *Plants with variegated leaves create color throughout summer and, if evergreen, the entire year. Many can be grown in pots and tubs.*

design inspirations

The choice of styles for your garden is wide and these range from English flower gardens to patios and courtyards which are ideal for creating outdoor living areas in space-restricted places. Pergolas, arches, and trellises can be used to create height as well as to provide seclusion and mystery, while arbours add romanticism to a garden. Paths, steps, walls, and fences are essential garden features and with careful planning these can be attractive as well as functional.

making the most of your soil

Soil can be slowly improved by adding well-decayed manure or garden compost, but more instant ways to create a colorful garden are to select plants that survive the conditions in the garden being planted. It is inevitable, however, that gardeners will wish to grow other kinds of plants.

Raised beds

Where the ground is continually moist and drainage is difficult, or if the soil is exceptionally chalky or acid, construct a raised bed 12–18in/30–45cm high and fill it with good soil. This enables a wide range of plants to grow. Use cascading plants at the sides to cloak the edges.

Preparing planting areas

Where the soil is exceptionally dry or of poor quality, small areas can be improved to enable climbers and other plants to be grown. Dig out the soil from an area about 2ft/60cm square and deep, and fill the lower 4in/10cm with rubble. Top up with good topsoil, and firm it. Put in the plant and water the area regularly until it is established. Do not plant climbers less than 1ft/30cm from a wall, because the soil is always fairly dry close to a wall.

Growing acid-loving plants

Most soils are only slightly acid and can be improved by dusting the surface with hydrated lime or ground limestone each winter. It is better to grow acid-loving plants such as callunas and heathers on soils that are strongly acid and formed mainly of peat or peat substitute. There are many varieties of these plants. Some have attractive foliage and others are grown for their flowers. Many varieties flower through cold winter months. Azaleas can be planted in lightly shaded

◀ *When there is a problem with the soil, a raised bed is an ideal solution. It also enables plants to be seen and reached easily.*

areas with slighlty acid soils to create a spectacular spring display.

Growing chalk-loving plants

It is more difficult to correct chalky soils than acid types. Acidic fertilizers, such as sulfate of ammonia, can be used with additions of peat substitute, but if the underlying soil is alkaline it is better to grow only chalk-loving plants. A raised bed is the best solution for gardeners with acid soil and an irrepressible desire to grow chalk-loving plants.

Wet and boggy areas

Many soils with a high water level can be drained, enabling a wide range of plants to be grown. However, if the area is naturally wet, difficult to drain, and perhaps close to a stream, it is better to plant moisture-loving plants. They include *Lysichiton americanus* (skunk cabbage) with bright yellow, arum-like flower heads in spring, and its near relative *Lysichiton camtschatcensis*, with pure white flowers. Along the sides of streams plant shrubs such as *Cornus stolonifera* 'Flaviramea' and *C. alba* 'Sibirica' for their colored winter stems.

Hot, dry soils

Gardening successfully on hot, dry soils depends on three factors: mixing in bulky materials such as well-rotted manure and garden compost annually, to aid water retention; regular watering; and adding a mulch each spring. Selecting plants that survive in hot, dry soils is also important (see pages 42–43).

Pots, tubs, and other containers

Some soils are so inhospitable that plants cannot be grown easily. This problem is best solved by planting a wide range of plants in containers. They range from pots and tubs to window boxes, hanging baskets, troughs, and wall baskets. Buying, planting and looking after plants in containers is more expensive and involves more work than caring for plants in borders and beds. However, it does provide you with the opportunity to recreate your garden, which can be an advantage.

▲ To bring color through the year, plant large pots with dwarf or slow-growing conifers and position them along the edges of a path.

▼ Cloak the sides of a natural stone wall in plants. They may grow in the wall or be planted at its foot. Planted pots are an alternative.

gardening on slopes

Sloping ground offers an opportunity to create an unusual garden, but it will be more expensive to develop than a flat site. A number of paved, terraced areas around a house make an attractive feature when the ground slopes downward from the house.

▲ *A paved area halfway up a slope creates an exciting yet practical leisure area, especially when it features a pond and a fountain.*

Terraced gardens

A garden may be terraced in formal or informal style, depending partly on the style of the house. Formal terraces connected by flights of steps usually suit modern houses. Cottages demand an informal style. A slope dotted with fruit trees is an attractive feature.

Paved areas

When a house stands at the bottom of a facing slope, a flat, paved area can usually be laid at the base of the slope. An alternative is to create a paved area about one-third of the way up the slope to break up the degree of incline. Where possible, position the area so that it is easily visible from the ground floor of the house, so that people do not have to look sharply up to see it.

Where the ground falls away from the house, lay a flat, paved area as near to the house as possible. Meandering paths can be laid to lead downward from it, perhaps criss-crossing the slope to make them appear less steep and easier to use. These paved areas need not be central but off to one side, which particularly suits informal gardens. Where the end of a garden rises, lay a paved area and erect a summerhouse on top. Check that the neighbors will not think it an intrusion on their privacy.

Retaining walls

These are invariably constructed across slopes to retain banks of soil up to 4ft/1.2m high. Some walls are formal, perhaps built from bricks or blocks, while others are made of natural stone. These are particularly suitable for planting *Aurinia saxatilis* (still better known as *Alyssum saxatile*) and aubrieta. By positioning

wide paths along the base of informal retaining walls the plants can be admired without being damaged. Formal retaining walls, especially when made of brick, do not need a wide path alongside them. However, if a lawn is positioned close to them, construct a mowing strip at the base to enable a lawn mower to cut as close to the wall as possible.

Sloping woodland and wild gardens

Old railroad ties are ideal for retaining soil on steep slopes in rustic areas. Secure the ties in position, using strong wooden posts or metal spikes. Beds of heathers and deciduous azaleas create superb

displays on slopes. Logs can create an attractive and natural edging that especially harmonizes with informal gardens. Use several strong, wooden stakes to secure them in position and pack well-drained, friable soil along the inside edge.

Lawn banks

Traditionally, especially on large country estates, slopes were terraced and grassed, with 45° slopes separating level areas 10–12ft/3–3.6m wide. These dramatic features can easily be replicated on a smaller scale in formal gardens. The key is to keep it all in proportion.

▲ *Flights of steps create visually exciting features in gardens. Insure that they are soundly constructed and have all-weather surfaces.*

◄ *Slopes are ideal places for a series of waterfalls. If these cover a large area, a reservoir tank may be needed at the top.*

aspect, light, and shade

The range of trees, shrubs, herbaceous perennials, annuals, and other garden plants is wide, and there are types for all aspects and intensities of light or shade. Some of these extremes can be lessened by planting or cutting down trees, but it is usually a matter of learning to live with your garden.

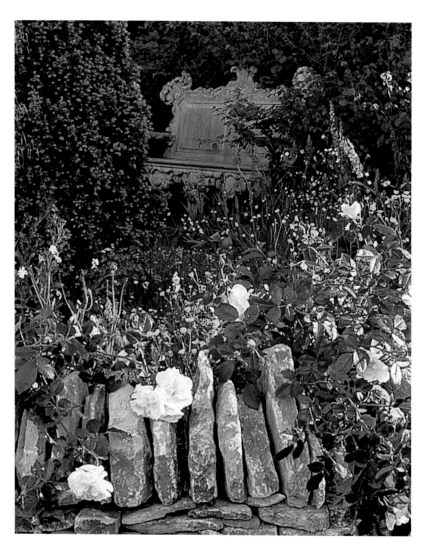

◄ *A shady border can bloom as brightly as a sunny border. Plants with colorful flowers and attractive leaves will grow in all garden areas.*

The lottery of aspect

A garden's aspect is not usually the first consideration when buying a house. Rather, it is one of the lotteries of gardening. Cold, searing wind is a problem for some plants, while strong, intense sunlight causes difficulties for many. All gardens have possibilities and limitations, and there are plants for even the most inhospitable places. This book explores many ideas that will make growing plants easy. For example, pages 42–43 suggest plants for hot, sunny areas and advise on growing them, and shade-loving plants are on pages 44–45.

Coastal considerations

Coastal gardens are at risk from several factors. Cold, strong, buffeting winds may deform trees and shrubs, especially in winter, and the salt-laden wind will damage leaves and flowers. It is essential to create windbreaks and hedges to filter the wind and reduce its speed, especially in gardens close to the sea. However, there are plenty of hardy plants that will thrive in coastal areas.

Winter wonderlands

In some areas, winter weather is so harsh that the likelihood of growing flowers is dramatically reduced. However, several hardy trees flower during winter and they include *Hamamelis mollis* (Chinese witch hazel) and *Cornus mas* (Cornelian cherry). Bear in mind that frost forms attractive patterns on leaves, while a light dusting of snow can be attractive.

In exceptionally cold areas, a layer of snow helps insulate bulbs against low temperatures, but where possible remove snow carefully from the leaves of evergreen shrubs before it weighs them down and disfigures the branches.

▲ Steps strongly constructed and recessed in a retaining wall are attractive, and give ready access to the border behind.

▼ An ornamental pond needs to be positioned in good light and where leaves will not litter the water through the fall.

english flower gardens

Few gardening styles are as relaxed and informal as an English country garden. Herbaceous borders are packed with plants that mostly die down to soil level in the fall, and develop fresh shoots and leaves in spring. Mixed borders are a medley of plants, including shrubs and bulbs.

▲ *The fleshy-rooted border perennial agapanthus creates a mass of large, umbrella-shaped flower heads mainly during mid- and late summer.*

Herbaceous borders

During the late 1800s the Irish garden writer William Robinson (1838–1935) published *The English Flower Garden*, in which he enthused about herbaceous perennials. He claimed that the English cottage had for many years been a repository for herbaceous plants. His writings came at a time when there was a general hunger for information about plants, and a popularization of gardening books and magazines. However, Gertrude Jekyll (1843–1932) is the best-known advocate of herbaceous plants. Her first book about these plants, *Wood and Garden*, appeared in 1899, followed by others that included ideas about single-color borders. Pages 70–77 explain color-themed borders, including pink and red, blue and mauve, yellow and gold, and white and silver plants.

Mixed borders

Few small gardens can have more than a corner devoted to a color-themed border, so tend to display a mixture of herbaceous perennials, bulbs, annuals, shrubs, and trees producing a rich array of colors, sizes, and shapes. Such borders create a good opportunity to have all the plants you like.

Hardy and half-hardy annuals are excellent space fillers during the early years of a mixed border. The half-hardy annuals are planted in gaps in early summer, as soon as all risk of frost has passed, while hardy annuals can be sown earlier. Always sow the seeds of hardy annuals thinly.

Bulbs provide extra color and include lilies that delight in soil shaded and cooled by other plants. Clumps of trumpet-type daffodils are very welcome in early spring and, although they leave a legacy of untidy leaves during early summer, they are rich in color.

Hardy annual borders

If you have a passion for bright colors which you can change each year, think of planting a border of hardy annuals. A few packets of seeds will produce glorious displays of color for months on end. However, be careful not to sow seeds too early in the year. They will not germinate if the soil is not warm enough, and they may start to decay if conditions are too wet.

In windy areas, select moderately tall hardy annuals, and support them with twiggy sticks. A few annuals have special appeal to children, particularly *Helianthus annuus*, the sunflower, which has large flowers often as wide as 12in/30cm wide. Some grow as high as 10ft/3m, although others are much shorter, and these varieties are ideal for windy sites. Sunflowers are easy to grow in a sunny position and look especially attractive against a white wall that highlights the yellow petals and brown or purple centers.

▲ Use relatively low-growing and lax flowering plants to create bright edges to paths, especially where informality is desired.

◄ Floriferous herbaceous borders, with their relaxed and informal nature, have been a traditional part of English gardens.

HARDY ANNUALS FOR ROCK GARDENS

Even in a small garden hardy annuals have a useful role, especially in rock gardens where they fill bare areas and add extra color. Plants to choose from include:
• *Adonis annua* (pheasant's eye) – 10in/25cm high with deep crimson flowers with black centers.
• *Limnanthes douglasii* (Poached egg plant) – 6in/15cm high with bright white flowers with yellow centers.

informal gardens

Informal gardens appeal to many gardeners because they have a more restful atmosphere than more regimented gardens with plants in straight lines and borders in geometric shapes. Cottage gardens are the epitome of informality because plants of many types grow together in a relaxed way.

Cottage gardens

To many gardeners, the key features of cottage gardens are secluded bowers, rustic trellises with scented climbers and beds patchworked with flowers, fruit, and vegetables. There is even space for topiary birds and animals trained in *Taxus* (yew) and *Ligustrum* (privet). Armillary spheres, with their circular arrangement of rings showing the relative positions of celestial bodies, are less formal than sundials, and add to the relaxed atmosphere.

To ensure an authentic cottage garden, you can also grow apple varieties with wonderful flavors. They include 'McIntosh,' 'Gold Rush,' 'Rome,' 'Newtown Pippin,' and 'Spartan'. Good pear varieties include 'Comice', 'Harrow Delight', 'Harvest Queen,' and 'Stark Honeysweet'. Pole beans (*Phaseolus vulgaris*) on tripods in borders add height and create a background for other plants.

Wild gardens

Wild gardens are not a contradiction in terms but a way of bringing a hint of the wild landscape into a small, controlled environment. A light, overhead canopy of trees helps to create shade for plants from *Hyacinthoides* (bluebell) to azaleas. If you have inherited a garden with deeper shade you can alleviate the conditions by thinning branches, but in any case stick to shade-loving plants (see pages 44–45). Other features to include are meandering rustic paths linking garden areas, and alpine "meadows" with low-growing bulbous plants in short grass. These are lovely in full sun, especially on a slope.

◄ *Benches and other seats are an essential feature in a garden, since they create places from which it can be admired.*

Wild flowers are also necessary to attract a wide range of insects. Many seed companies sell special mixtures of wild flowers and they are best sown in the spring. Most will reseed themselves during the following year and, although not all gardeners will wish to create such informal areas, they constitute an environmentally friendly way of keeping a healthy garden.

Soothing sounds

Most gardens have colorful flowers and attractive foliage, but why not add comforting sounds as a new dimension? These can range from the rustling of leaves to the reassuring pitter-patter of water splashing and tumbling from fountains or bubbling along in streams. Some plants are especially known for their ability to create sound in even the

slightest breeze. Grasses and bamboos rustle, as do the leaves of some trees, and a gravel path with bamboos on either side is a sight and sound to enjoy throughout the year. Encourage birds and birdsong with a bird bath or a feeding area well out of the reach of cats. Continue feeding the birds in winter, but do not leave whole peanuts, hard fat, or too much bread in early spring when there may be young in the nests.

WIND CHIMES

Wind chimes suspended from trees close to a house add a gentle and comforting sound to the garden. However, do not put them where they may cause irritation through being repeatedly knocked.

▲ *A stream meandering through a wild flower garden is a captivating feature. A bench is a resting point from which plants may be admired.*

▼ *Wild flower gardens are easily created and mixtures of wild flower seeds are available from seed companies. Always sow the seeds thinly.*

formal gardens

Formally designed gardens appeal to many gardeners. They provide a neat appearance and a better opportunity than informal types to change arrangements of plants from spring to summer, as well as from one year to another. Small front gardens often have a formal design.

Carpet bedding

During the mid-1800s many low-growing, subtropical plants were introduced into gardens, and by the 1870s they were grown to form carpets of color in borders. Most were planted in geometric patterns, but some formed monograms, especially in large estates.

The art of carpet bedding spread to botanical and municipal gardens, and towns competed to create the most

▲ *Formal gardens have a clinical nature that suits many small areas. Ponds, either round or square, create attractive features.*

original and attractive display. Some designs of carpet bedding were even used as advertisements, as commemorative notices, and to depict the names of towns. Carpet bedding is still widely practiced in formal parks, the centers of large cities, and in popular coastal resorts.

Home gardeners pursue this type of gardening by growing half-hardy annuals in summer, and bulbs and biennials in spring and the fall.

Summer displays

Plant summer bedding displays in late spring or early summer, as soon as all risk of damage from frost has passed. The plants are raised from seeds sown in late winter or early spring in gentle warmth in greenhouses, and are later acclimatized to outdoor conditions. As well as half-hardy annuals, plants with attractive foliage are also used and they range from *Bassia scoparia trichophylla* better known as *Kochia trichophylla* (burning bush, summer cypress) and *Euphorbia marginata* 'Snow on the mountain' to *Abutilon pictum*

'Thompsonii'. They are often used as "dot" plants to create height in an otherwise low display.

Plants traditionally used in formal bedding displays include *Lobularia maritima*, still known as *Alyssum maritimum* (sweet alyssum), bushy forms of *Lobelia erinus* in colors including blue, white, and red, and the many forms of *Tagetes* (marigold).

Spring displays

Early bedding displays usually contain a medley of biennials and spring-flowering bulbs, especially tulips. Biennials are sown in nursery beds in late spring or early summer, and are planted in borders in late summer or early fall. Bulbs such as tulips are planted at the same time.

Spring displays can be a rich mix of colors, shapes, and heights and include biennials such as *Bellis perennis* (English daisy), wallflowers, *Dianthus barbatus* (sweet William) and *Myosotis sylvatica* (forget-me-not). In late spring or early summer, after their display has finished, the plants are pulled up. The soil is then forked over, lightly firmed by shuffling over it, and planted with summer-flowering displays.

Knot gardens

The knot garden was once an expression of the unchanging, endless nature of life. By the mid-1600s "knot garden" had become a term to describe a flower garden surrounded by and interwoven with paths. Today, it is associated with miniature hedges of *Buxus sempervirens* 'Suffruticosa' (edging boxwood) surrounding small flower beds. These intricate shapes are ideal in small gardens.

Formal ponds

Round ponds are simple but distinctive, especially when they feature a fountain. They need a formal setting, perhaps in a wide lawn surrounded, at a distance, by a formal hedge of *Taxus baccata* (English yew). Alternatively, lay wide paths around the pond and divide the surrounding space into four separate garden areas planted with summer-flowering bedding plants. Use containers to create height.

FORMAL TOPIARY

Unlike topiary animals and birds, which are traditional in cottage gardens, topiary cones, pyramids, and squares may be more suited to formal areas. These can be grouped, perhaps towards the end of a formal lawn, or dotted around a garden.

▶ *Miniature hedges grown from edging boxwood are ideal for encircling a border. They create formality without dominating the garden.*

paths for all gardens

Paths should not just be ribbon-like features providing quick access from one part of a garden to another, they should be attractive in their own right, with surfaces that harmonize with the rest of the garden. These pages explore the many different construction materials available for paths.

Why have a path?

Paths are essential in many parts of a garden. An all-weather surface right around a house is especially necessary to link it with a garage, fuel store, and sheds. But even these domestic demands do not mean that a path need be featureless and unimaginative. Areas around cottages can have gray, ribbed-surfaced paving stones spaced 4in/10cm apart in a sea of gravel, or a natural stone path with spaces for low plants. Modern houses need a more formal style, which may be provided by a wide range of plain or mixed surfaces. It is, fortunately, no longer necessary to lay a path alongside a clothes line, thanks to the introduction of compact clothes lines which rotate on a single pole.

Constraints and opportunities

The choice of materials for the construction of a path is influenced by the garden's topography and shape.

▶ *Crazy-paving paths are right for flat and for sloping gardens because they can hug closely to the most twisting and undulating contours.*

Materials such as square or rectangular paving slabs are ideal for straight paths, whereas crazy paving is more adaptable and can be used for straight and for curved paths. Grass paths, with or without stepping stones running down the center, may be curved or straight, while informal paths of thyme look particularly eye-catching when in flower.

A garden that is undulating or markedly sloped has a strong influence on the selection of materials. Crazy paving is perfectly suited to ground that slopes in several directions, whereas formal paths are best where the slope is in one direction. Gravel paths should be reserved for flat areas because the gravel inevitably migrates slowly downhill.

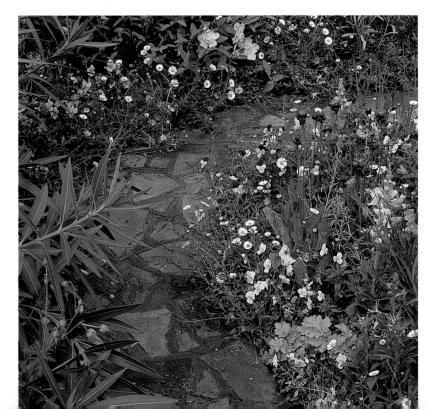

Materials used to construct a path should be in proportion to its width. A path formed of a combination of small, rectangular and square paving slabs looks out of proportion if over 2ft/60cm wide. For a wider path use larger paving slabs. Conversely, narrow paths of crazy paving appear confusing, but look better when wider and irregularly shaped.

Medley paths

Paths can be formed of several different materials. Those for informal areas could include cross-slices of tree trunks positioned as stepping stones in a sea of coarse gravel, or six-sided concrete slabs with pebbles, while railroad ties spaced 3–4in/7.5–10cm apart in cobbles or gravel also work well. In wild gardens, make gravel or grass paths edged with logs, and in rural gardens where borders are wide, use sections of logs as stepping stones to give access to the entire area.

For formal gardens, the range of materials is much wider. Make patterns from paving slabs of different shapes but similar texture and color, with gaps left for cobbles, but remember that this may make the path very uneven. Bricks and flexible pavers can also be laid in attractive patterns.

WINTER WARNING

Where plants are positioned in gaps between paving slabs, do not use salt to remove ice, or use a shovel or spade to scrape away snow. Instead, let them melt naturally.

▲ Informal paths formed of a well-drained but firm base covered with shredded bark and with a low, woven edging are ideal for rustic gardens.

▼ Concrete pavers are right for straight paths in formal gardens. The pavers can be laid in straight lines or in complex patterns.

walls and fences

Most gardens have a wall or a fence to define boundaries, create privacy, deflect noise, and screen unpleasant views. The main constructional difference is that a wall needs strong foundations along its entire length, whereas a fence requires support only for the concrete or wooden posts.

◄ *Walls of all types, formal or informal, create secluded and cloistered spots which may have small paved areas for garden furniture.*

Fence or wall?

Brick walls are much more expensive to construct than fences. A wall 6ft/1.8m high needs to be 9in/23cm thick, with strengthening piers every 6ft/1.8m. Even screen-block walling (blocks 12in/30cm square and 4in/10cm thick, with a latticework design) needs strong foundations and piers every 10ft/3m, and supports at the ends. Screen-block walling can be combined attractively with a traditional brick wall or with bricks of reconstituted stone.

Fences range from white picket fencing to close-boarding. The framework of a close-boarded fence is built from 4–6in/10–15cm wide pales (strips of wood) nailed to arris rails. Such fences are usually 4ft/1.2m to 6ft/1.8m high. Always select a fence to harmonize with the garden. For example, a picket fence is ideal for the front boundary of a

cottage garden, whereas wattle fencing and chestnut paling are better suited for the back area. Panel fencing, with 6ft/1.8m long panels from 4ft/1.2m to 6ft/1.8m high, is popular and somewhat cheaper than close-boarding.

Low-slung post and chain fencing is ideal for marking a boundary, but it will not keep people out. The chain is now usually made of strong plastic and needs no maintenance. Ranch-style fencing, with planks of wood 6–8ft/1.8–2.4m long and 6–8in/15–20cm wide nailed to posts, has a modern, open feel. Gaps of about 4in/10cm are left between the planks, but to stop people looking through, nail planks on alternate sides of the supporting posts which are concreted into the ground. These fences can be 3ft/90cm to 6ft/1.8m high.

Cast-iron fencing is ideal for surrounding the front gardens of Victorian, Georgian, and other period town houses. This kind of fence is usually 3–6ft/90cm–1.8m high and painted black. The fences are very attractive and can be used as features on their own, or underplanted with a range of colorful flowers and leafy plants.

Gates for all gardens

Walls and fences in front gardens are not complete without a complementary gate. White picket fences need rustic wooden gates while an old, weathered brick wall with an arch requires a wrought-iron gate with a round top.

The range of decorative patterns in wrought-iron gates is wide, and this is usually reflected in the cost. Wooden gates vary in style, and apart from the paling type there are overlapping board gates and those which feature diamond-slatted cladding.

▼ *Choose a fence that suits your garden. Wattle fencing panels secured to stout posts are informal and rustic, and right for a cottage garden style.*

THIEF-PROOF GATES

Wrought-iron gates are usually hung on peg hinges and can be stolen quickly and easily. To prevent this happening, secure the lower hinge to the post and with the peg upward, hang the gate and secure the top hinge with the peg downward. Now the gate cannot be lifted off. Wooden gates are usually more secure as the hinge is screwed to the gate and the supporting post.

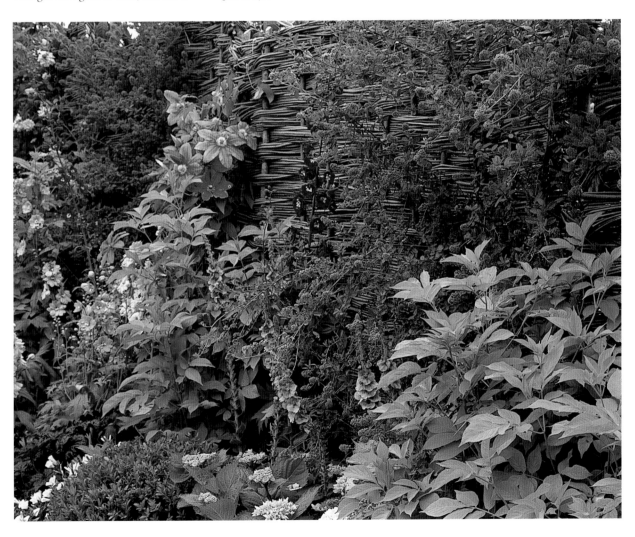

steps for all gardens

Handsome flights of steps that harmonize with the rest of the garden become enduring features of interest. They must, of course, be functional, but there is no reason why they cannot also be attractive. Here is a range of steps that will enhance your garden, whatever its style or size.

Informal steps

Log steps are essential for wild gardens on slopes. Thick logs or old railroad ties can be used to form the risers. They have a relaxing appearance and can be enhanced by daffodils naturalized in the grass beside them. Instead of forming narrow ribbons of daffodils, plant them in wide groups, about one-third the width of the steps.

In small areas, consider naturalizing *Crocus chrysanthus* bulbs alongside a path. They flower in late winter and early spring and in a wide range of colors including yellow, blue, and bronze.

Consider planting trees on either side of narrow, informal steps set in a steep bank. This will create a light canopy of branches and leaves. Grass steps look good in informal and semiformal gardens. Log steps with grass forming the treads are also informal, but they are not all-weather surfaces. For long flights of steps, a strimmer is essential for cutting the grass, whereas in small areas a pair of hedging shears is sufficient. Semiformal grass steps use bricks at the edges of the treads, with grass behind them.

Formal steps

Large, wide flights of steps, especially those with wide areas at the top and base, make dominant features. Narrow steps can also be attractive in small gardens, especially when built with unusual materials. Bricks with a

▲ *A flight of garden steps, especially when constructed from attractive natural materials, creates a pleasing feature.*

chamfered edge can be used as part of the tread, with other bricks as the risers. Steps with a semicircular design and a full circle of bricks at the top, are very attractive and always capture attention. The inner parts of the treads can be formed using colored gravels, bricks, or grass. Semicircular steps work well as a link between patio or terrace and grass lawn, and between different levels of grass, but do not attempt to form large flights of these steps; usually, three steps on a slight slope is sufficient.

▼ *Wrought iron spiral staircases create unusual features, either in basement gardens or, when shortened, as steps to a different level.*

RECYCLING SPIRAL STAIRCASES

Old spiral staircases are very decorative and can be used in basement gardens as a feature. They look good when cloaked in small-leaved *Hedera* (ivy), with supporting pots and small hanging baskets.

shady patios

We owe the term "patio" to the Spanish, who used it to describe an inner courtyard, surrounded by a dwelling and open to the sky. Patios are an integral part of the house, providing shade and shelter throughout the day, and they were traditionally planted with leafy plants and colorful flowers.

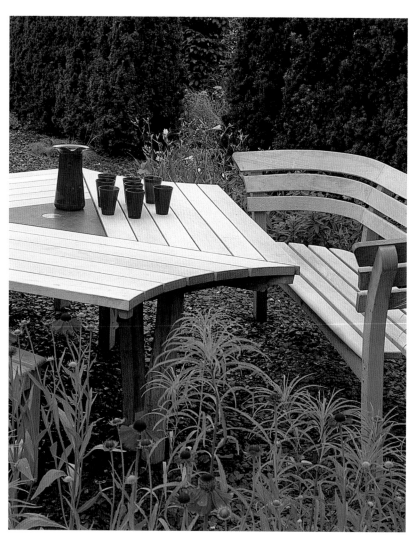

◄ *A secluded patio, shaded from strong sunlight, is an oasis of calm. Tables and benches are essential for outdoor living.*

Publicizing patios

The concept of patios spread from Spain to the southern United States and then westward to California, where they were ideally suited to the climate. Later, the term migrated to the temperate regions of Europe, where it is often now used instead of the word terrace.

The L-shaped patio

Many houses have an L-shaped area outside a rear entrance, and it can be partly enclosed by a fence. An alternative is to use a free-standing trellis, erected about 18in/45cm from the boundary, and with one end forming an L-shape, to create an even more cloistered area. To make an evergreen screen of foliage, erect a trellis and plant a large-leaved variegated ivy such as *Hedera colchica* 'Sulphur Heart' or *H. c.* 'Dentata Variegata'. Both have variegated leaves.

For summer foliage the herbaceous climber *Humulus lupulus* 'Aureus' (Hops) creates a handsome screen of leaves. Where a flowering screen is desired, plant *Clematis montana*.

Surfacing patios

An attractive, well-drained surface is essential. It need not be consistent across the entire patio because you can leave spaces for shrubs and small trees. Other areas can be laid with cobbles, with large containers standing on top.

Paving slabs with raised patterns, brick-like slabs positioned together to create a pattern, and granite setts can all be used, but do avoid smooth, highly colored and checkerboard surfaces.

Healing nature

Part of the enchantment of a patio is the opportunity to have cool, refreshing water splashing from a fountain into a central pond. Repetitive but irregular

gentle sound has a therapeutic effect that helps to reduce stress. Also, an enclosed patio stops the scent of plants from being blown away. *Helichrysum serotinum* (curry plant) may well trigger memories of a visit to Asia, while the unforgettable perfume of lilac may conjure up thoughts of a wedding bouquet. Many

fragrances are more personal. A mistress of the novelist H. G. Wells claimed that his body emitted a honey-like fragrance. She could have recaptured this with the honey-scented bulbs *Crocus chrysanthus* or *Iris danfordiae*. Both can be grown beside paths and also in containers such as pots and window boxes.

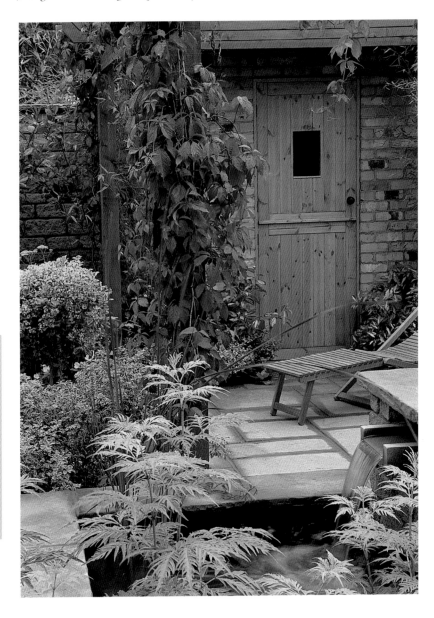

ORNAMENTS ON PATIOS

Small statuary and ornamental pots are ideal for creating interest on patios. Large, barrel-like pots make superb homes for *Clematis macropetala*, with its tangled mass of stems and double blue flowers during late spring and early summer. It has the bonus of producing silky, fluffy seedheads.

▶ *An ornamental pond has calming, therapeutic qualities which help to reduce stress, making it a perfect feature for a patio.*

sunny terraces

A terrace is an open and usually paved area connecting a house with its garden. It usually has a balustrade or a low wall, especially if raised above the level of the garden. Many houses and bungalows have a flat, all-weather surface like a terrace at the back which may be used to create an outdoor leisure area.

Ancient heritage

Terraced landscapes with superb views were known in Thebes, Egypt, in about 1500 BCE. This style of gardening progressed westward to Italy, where terraces were created as status and power symbols, while giving views over the surrounding countryside. During the Middle Ages the viewing equivalent of a terrace was constructed on castle walls, while in 13th-century Spain the gardens on the hill slopes of the Alhambra had similar constructions. The English landscape designer Humphry Repton (1752–1818) was very keen on terracing, and in 18th-century England a variation known as the terrace walk became popular, with a surface of grass rather than paving. Such terraces were often long and especially sited to give views of the surrounding landscape. Grassed terraces were either straight or gently curved.

Versatile terraces

Most paved areas in temperate climates are terraces. They are usually adjacent to a house, open to the sky and, where possible, positioned to gain the maximum sun (unlike patios, which are features of hot countries where shade is essential). The surface of terraces varies from natural stone paving, ideal for areas around cottages, to paving slabs that suit modern demands. Natural stone paving can be made even more informal by planting prostrate plants between the irregular-sized slabs. For formal terraces that dominate a garden, choose brightly colored, smooth-surfaced slabs perhaps laid in a checkerboard fashion. For other formal areas where plants are cherished as much as they are on the patio, use less dramatically colored slabs, perhaps with a ribbed surface.

Large terraces are still sometimes built and include raised beds. Plant them

◀ *South-facing terraces bask in sun through the summer. A garden pond with a fountain give eye-catching movement and cool the air on hot days.*

with shrubs and small trees to provide some shade. Tubs, ornamental stone sinks, pots, window boxes, and troughs are other worthwhile features.

Balustrades and walls

In Classical times, terraces had carved stone balustrades. Today, these can be superb features around the edge of a terrace, giving it a hint of Classical style. This type of feature is most appropriate for more formal architecture. Balustrades in this style are totally unsuited to a modern, brightly colored area, for which a wall partly formed of screen blocks with a concrete capping is much more

appropriate. Bear in mind that safety is a priority along the edge of a terrace on a steep slope, especially when young children are likely to use the area. A wall about 2½ft/75cm high is essential. Wooden balustrades are seldom seen, although a form of ranch-style fencing about 2½ft/75cm high suits terraces surfaced with brightly colored, smooth-surfaced paving slabs. They can be painted white, and built even higher if privacy is an important consideration.

▼ All-weather surfaces for terraces are essential. They should slope away from the house a little so torrential rain can drain away.

▲ Where sunlight is strong throughout summer, attach canopies to the top of patio windows. Insure that they can be taken down in the fall.

courtyards

Courtyards have a history that extends back more than 1,000 years. They have long been a key functional area in forts and castles, and they were built into the palaces of the Moslem rulers of Arabia, North Africa, and Spain, where they provided pleasant relief from the heat of the sun.

Shady and secluded

Today, courtyards in town gardens are usually small, secluded, and protected from strong wind, although where gates are on the north side there is a risk of cold winter winds searing the foliage of evergreen plants. Courtyards always have shady areas but this need not be a problem as many plants, including ferns, grow in shade and moist soil (see pages 44–45). You can also grow almost anything, from small trees to bulbs in containers placed to catch the sun.

Seclusion and shade appeal to many gardeners, especially in towns where privacy is hard to find. Shade from strong sun is welcome during the day, but in the late evening the gloom may make the area too dark to use. One solution is to have spotlights and concealed lighting fitted by a qualified electrician.

Basement apartments sometimes have cloistered areas. These can be

treated as courtyards, and decorated with plants in containers. If they have stone steps connecting them with ground level, these can be made more attractive by planting trailing plants such as variegated forms of *Vinca minor* (lesser periwinkle), beside them. Plant it toward the top of the steps, so it can trail freely downward. The prostrate *Lysimachia nummularia* (creeping Jenny) will also brighten the edges of steps, and grows

well in partial shade. For extra color choose the form 'Aurea' with yellow leaves. However, this variety does not thrive in deep shade.

Flooring a courtyard

A wide variety of paving materials is suitable for courtyards. Large, aged, well-worn flagstones are ideal, but they can be difficult to obtain and are usually expensive. Alternatives are brick pavers,

▶ *Courtyards have a secluded and often partly shaded nature. Use plants in pots and tubs and select those that thrive in shaded areas.*

granite setts, and reconstituted flagstones. Cobbles are another possibility but they are difficult to walk on.

Furniture and gates for courtyards

Wrought-iron or aluminum furniture with an aged, ornate appearance suits a cloistered, shady courtyard. Besides harmonizing with the walls, nonferrous metal furniture does not deteriorate, although it is usually necessary to scrub off lichen and moss in spring. Wooden

furniture, such as conjoined benches and tables, are always much in demand. In late fall stand each leg on a brick, and cover the entire table with a plastic sheet tied down securely to protect it from winter weather. Collapsible, slatted furniture has the advantage that it can be taken indoors and stored. Ornate wrought-iron gates make ideal entrances to courtyard gardens. They are not as dominant as wooden doors and allow the outside world to be seen at a glance.

▲ *Courtyards are not complete without furniture; wrought iron is ideal for these small areas because it takes up little space and can often be folded for storage.*

EARLY MOTELS

In the Near and Far East caravanserais, or caravansary, have been known for many centuries. These were caravan hostels for merchants and travellers built around a large courtyard.

pergolas, arches, and trellises

Structures like pergolas were known in warm countries from the earliest times. In Egypt they were probably used to support vines and create shade. The Italians took up the idea and came up with the term "pergola," meaning an arbor, bower, or a walk of bowers covered mainly with vines.

Pergolas for all places

Pergolas can be informal, formal, or even oriental. Those constructed from rustic poles, often astride paths, are ideal for giving support to leafy climbers such as *Vitis vinifera*. The leaf shapes look more informal than the leaves of the ordinary vine. If an informal flowering and highly fragrant climber is desired, choose *Lonicera periclymenum* 'Belgica' (early Dutch honeysuckle) or *L. p.* 'Serotina' (late Dutch honeysuckle). *Lonicera japonica* (Japanese honeysuckle) also has a free-flowing show of flowers.

Formal pergolas formed of planed timber, with square-cut uprights and crossbeams, make ideal supports for wisteria. Although wisteria can be grown against a house wall, it is better where the large bunches of flowers can hang freely. It is a vigorous climber, so it soon drains the border soil around a house of any moisture, which can be detrimental to the house and to other plants growing alongside it.

An oriental look can be given to formal pergolas by cutting the underside edges and ends of the crossbeams at a sloping angle. Lean-to pergolas are another variation and can be made to look like an arbor if climbing plants are trained around uprights and crossbeams. Proprietary brackets are available for securing the crossbeams to a wall, with wooden uprights on the other side.

◀ *Most pergolas are straight and straddle paths, but an alternative use is to enclose a rounded area, perhaps devoted to growing bush roses.*

Arches

At their simplest, arches are just inverted hoops over a path covered in climbers, from roses to the leafy herbaceous climber *Humulus lupulus* 'Aureus' (Hops). However, the ingenuity of gardeners has resulted in arches of all shapes and sizes, including four-way arches at the junctions of paths.

Use arches to create height and focal points, as well as to grow climbers. Metal arches are increasingly used to grow roses over paths and as features on lawns, where, covered in leafy plants, they take on the role of an arbor. Indeed, metal and wooden arches against a wall or a fence will create an attractive and romantic arbor.

Trellises

Trellises were traditionally secured to walls, but are increasingly used as a free-standing feature to provide privacy and to create smaller areas, each with a different atmosphere. They are also ideal for screening garbage cans.

Rose enthusiasts welcome free-standing trellis as an opportunity to grow more climbers. At the end of a broad lawn erect a line of trellis panels, with shorter panels at right-angles to them. This produces features resembling stalls for horses. Pillar roses, where both climbing and rambling-type roses are grown up rustic poles or tripods of sawn timber, can be integrated into the display to create a variety of shapes.

▲ Plants that reveal their flowers at eye-level create exciting gardens, with flowers and scent where they can be readily appreciated.

▼ Trellises attached to a wall make ideal homes for climbing roses, as well as for other climbers that require a supporting framework.

arbors and tunnels

Arbors and tunnels come in all shapes and sizes, and are mainly admired for their romantic, cloistered leafiness. Arbors are usually smothered in flowering and leafy climbers, while tunnels often have flowering or fruiting trees trained over a wooden or a metal structure.

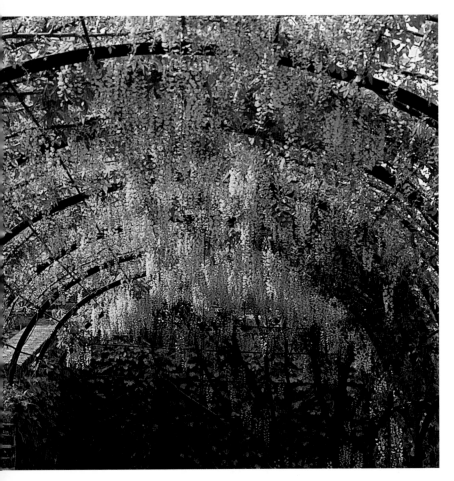

▲ *Laburnum trained over metal arches is awash with long, pendulous clusters of yellow flowers during late spring and early summer.*

Arbors for all gardens

There are arbors for all gardens. There are many suitable for small areas, where they fit into corners or alongside walls. Arbor units are increasingly sold either fully constructed or flat-packed, and are ready to erect, complete with a bench-style seat. Informal types are made of rustic poles, and formal ones of sawn timber. Some are made of wrought iron and have a delicate, aged look that suits roses and less vigorous climbers, such as *Clematis orientalis* (Oriental clematis), *C. tangutica* and *C. macropetala*.

An arbor in the center of a garden is an eye-catching feature. It needs a firm, paved base to provide an area for seats and chairs, and perhaps a small, low table. Some arbors are constructed on a base raised slightly above the surrounding area. This arrangement may suit a more formal garden. An informal arbor with a floor of natural stone paving, may look better if level with the ground. Crazy paving has a semiformal appearance and is also most suitable for an arbor at ground level.

Tunnels

Tunnels are ideal for channeling people from one part of a garden to another, and if a sundial, an ornamental well, or a seat is positioned at the far end of the tunnel, it creates an attractive focal point. A tunnel may have a decorative quality, especially when clothed in laburnum or climbing roses. Apples and pears may also be planted to clothe a series of metal hoops reminiscent of arches. Brambles were traditionally used to make fruiting tunnels. Nut walks were once also popular, but they did not rely for support on large wire hoops. Instead, the branches were pruned to form a kind of tunnel over a rustic path.

Do not make a tunnel long in a short garden, because its length will draw attention to the garden's lack of length. Because they are symmetrical, tunnels are often located in a central position. Where a garden is divided by a crosswise free-standing trellis, bisecting it with a tunnel divides the garden and leads the eye toward another part of it. Feature a herb garden at the end of a fruit tunnel. Alternatively, position a sundial or a seat as a focal point, with a circular gravel path around it with beds for the herbs.

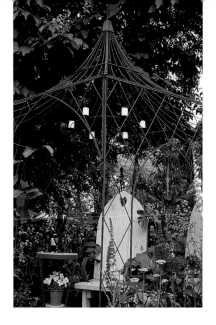

▲ A wrought iron framed gazebo is an open structure, perfect for climbing roses and for climbers with pendulous flowers.

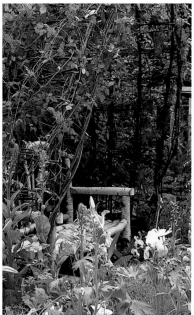

▲ Cloistered corners, heavily canopied with leafy and flowering climbers, can become secluded and romantic areas in gardens.

◄ A small gazebo is a striking structure, especially when positioned on a firm surface and nestling among shrubs and border plants.

porches and entrances

Porches prevent rain saturating people on arrival at a door. Large and ornate porches are often built around a front door, while less decorative and more functional types are at the rear. Rustic or formal arches can also be secured to walls around doors.

Brightening porches

A bare area around a front door gives an impression of lack of imagination, or neglect, but when a porch or a structure like a porch is fitted, it brightens the house and garden, especially when covered in leafy plants or flowers. Where a permanent brick-built structure is not possible, an arch may serve. Some may be bought for home assembly. Fit rustic arches around cottage doors and formal styles for more modern houses. Where extra weather protection is needed, secure an unobtrusive piece of wood to the top, to form a flat roof or one with a pitch. This will eventually be covered by the climber. Always secure the arch to the wall and insure that the four posts are concreted into the ground, so that they remain firm. The weight of climbers can be deceptively heavy, and winter winds may loosen weak fixtures.

The insides of large porches can be decorated with hanging baskets with drip trays in their base, and a bright show of tender plants. In summer they can range from *Campanula isophylla* (Star of Bethlehem) to *Chlorophytum comosum* 'Variegatum' (spider plant) and tradescantias. And in summer, the outside can be festooned with hanging baskets

◄ *Climbing plants enrich the outsides of entrances, creating a warm and friendly ambience in the garden and the house.*

suspended from brackets. Take care not to put them where the basket will be knocked, or where water will drip on to plants below. At ground level, hardy plants in containers can be left outside all year. They include narrow conifers, clipped box, and half-standard bay trees planted in tubs.

Not only can flowers and leafy plants make a porch more attractive inside and out but they can keep it colorful through the year. If you have a built porch, secure pieces of narrow trellis to the wall on either side of the door. Position each piece about 9in/23cm from the outer edge of the porch and plant variegated evergreens or plants that flower at different times of year to cover them.

Brightening gates and entrances

Front gardens bordered by a hedge such as a common privet or yew can be given a fresh identity by training branches to form an arch over a path. The training takes several years and is best performed on a tall hedge. Where paths are long, consider a metal or a wooden arch over the path, positioned about two-thirds of the way along it. Climbing roses clustered over metal arches are suitable for formal and informal areas. Arches constructed from rustic poles are strictly for cottage gardens and are ideal for supporting honeysuckle or jasmine.

Where there is not room for an arch, one or two pillar roses on either side of a path will introduce height to a garden.

▲ Small porches make a useful and attractive shelter from wind and rain. Linking them with a boundary fence creates a unified feature.

▼ Wrought iron gates and rustic entrances are especially attractive when roses or honeysuckle are trained over an arch.

39

creating your garden

Selecting features for a garden is one of the most exciting parts of gardening and these range from water gardens and colorful borders to secluded and scented corners that will delight you with a range of fragrances throughout the year. Bush and climbing roses are also possibilities, as well as paths formed of herbs. And whether you have a heavily shaded garden, or one that continually basks in sun, there are plenty of plants that will surprise you with their resilience.

gardening in full sun

Many plants, including hardy annuals, herbaceous perennials, and shrubs, grow well in strong sunlight. Unfortunately, hot sunshine inevitably means dry soil, but this is not an unsurmountable problem. A surprisingly large number of plants grow in these conditions.

Living with dry, hot soils

Full sun invariably means dry, impoverished soil unless provisions are made to improve it. These include digging in plenty of well-decayed garden compost or manure to increase the soil's ability to retain moisture. Also, watering the soil thoroughly and then adding a mulch 3in/7.5cm thick improves moisture retention and keeps the soil cool. In a rock garden or on a scree bed, a mulch of pea gravel or stone chippings will keep the soil cool and moist.

Hardy annuals for full sun

A few hardy annuals grow well in sun or partial shade, but some are especially at home in full sun. Adding well-decayed garden compost or manure to the soil in winter, followed by regular watering through the summer, are aids to success, particularly in hot, dry places. Sun-loving hardy annuals include the following:

- *Agrostemma githago* 'Milas' (corn-cockle)
- *Argemone mexicana* (prickly poppy)
- *Asperula orientalis* (woodruff)
- *Calendula officinalis* (pot marigold)
- *Carthamus tinctorius* (safflower)
- *Centaurea cyanus* (cornflower)
- *Eschscholzia californica* (California poppy)
- *Godetia amoena* (satin flower)
- *Gypsophila elegans* (baby's breath)
- *Helichrysum bracteatum* (strawflower)
- *Iberis amara* (rocket candytuft)
- *Limnanthes douglasii* (poached-egg flower)
- *Malope trifida* (annual mallow)
- *Nicandra physaloides* (shoo-fly)
- *Nigella damascena* (love-in-a-mist)
- *Phacelia campanularia* (California bluebell)
- *Scabiosa atropurpurea* (pincushion flower)

▶ Achillea *(yarrow) flourishes in strong sunlight and contrasts well with hollyhock, a hardy perennial usually grown as a biennial.*

Herbaceous plants for sunny borders

Because herbaceous perennials produce fresh leaves, stems, and flowers each year, they need to grow rapidly and without restriction from spring to fall. Many plants native to the Mediterranean region can survive in full sun with dry soil, especially those with silver leaves. Herbaceous perennials that survive in full sun and dry soil include:

- *Achillea millefolium* (yarrow)
- *Alstroemeria ligtu* 'Hybrids' (Peruvian lily)
- *Anaphalis margaritacea* (pearly everlasting)
- *Asphodeline lutea*
- *Baptisia australis* (plains false indigo)
- *Buphthalmum salicifolium* (willow-leaf ox-eye)
- *Catananche caerulea* (Cupid's dart)
- *Centaurea macrocephala*
- *Echinops ritro* (small globe thistle)
- *Eryngium* (sea holly)
- *Gypsophila paniculata* (baby's breath)
- *Heliopsis helianthoides scabra*
- *Limonium latifolium* (sea lavender)
- *Nepeta × faassenii* (catmint)
- *Solidago* (goldenrod)
- *Stachys byzantina* (lamb's ears)

Shrubs for dry, sunny borders

Thorough soil preparation is essential before planting shrubs for dry, sunny border. First-rate shrubs for full sun and dry soil include:

- *Artemisia abrotanum* (lad's love, southernwood)
- *Artemisia absinthium* (common wormwood)

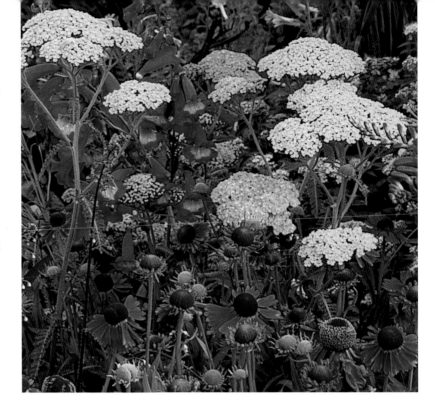

▲ *Achillea is an ideal herbaceous perennial for growing in a dry, sunny border. Its flowers are perfect for cutting and displaying indoors.*

- *Brachyglottis* 'Sunshine' (better known as *Senecio* 'Sunshine')
- *Buddleja davidii* (butterfly bush)
- *Caryopteris × clandonensis*
- *Ceratostigma willmottianum* (Chinese plumbago)

CONTAINER GARDENING

Container gardening is popular in hot, sunny countries and a wide range of sun-loving plants can be grown in pots, tubs, and window boxes. And if pots and tubs are put in groups, perhaps to one side of a patio, they can be watered more easily. Grouping containers in this way also helps keep them cooler than they would be if positioned separately. If pots and tubs at the back of a group are difficult to reach for watering, tie a stiff bamboo cane, 4ft/1.2m long to the end length of hose pipe so that you can hold it out.

- *Choisya ternata* (Mexican orange blossom)
- *Cistus* (rock rose)
- *Cytisus × praecox* 'Warminster' (Warminster broom)
- *Genista aetnensis* (Mount Etna broom)
- *Hebe speciosa* (shrubby veronica)
- *Helichrysum serotinum* (curry plant)
- *Kolkwitzia amabilis* (beauty bush)
- *Lavandula angustifolia* (lavender)
- *Lavatera* 'Rosea' (tree mallow)
- *Romneya coulteri* (tree poppy)
- *Rosmarinus officinalis* (rosemary)
- *Salvia officinalis* (common sage)—several colored leaf forms
- *Spartium junceum* (Spanish broom)

gardening in shade

Most gardens have a shady area, perhaps beside a house, a large tree, a fence, or a hedge. Such places can be a problem, but they also create opportunities to grow a wider range of plants. In fact, once established, many plants grow in shade, in dry, and moist soil.

Getting plants established

Plants in dry, shady areas are more difficult to establish than those in moisture-retentive soil. Dig dry areas thoroughly and mix in plenty of well-decayed garden compost or manure.

▲ *Many leafy plants thrive in shade. In this moist area,* Fatsia japonica *forms a perfect corner feature in a border and alongside a path.*

If the soil is impoverished, perhaps under trees or around the bases of shrubs, it will need a dusting of fertilizer. However, take care not to boost the growth of existing plants. Instead, add bonemeal to the planting hole, and a couple of times during the first year fork in a general fertilizer around the stem. Whatever happens, water plants regularly until they are established. Also lay a mulch, 3in/7.5cm thick around plants every spring. In moist, shady areas make sure that the soil is adequately drained by adding horticultural sand. The danger is that the plant roots may rot and die.

Plants for dry shade

Many highly attractive shrubs are sufficiently resilient to survive these conditions, and they include *Mahonia aquifolium* (Oregon grapeholly), which has leathery, glossy green leaves and fragrant, rich yellow flowers in spring. *Ruscus aculeatus* (butcher's broom) is another tough shrub. *Symphoricarpos* (snowberry) and osmanthus are other suitable shrubs. Good herbaceous

perennials include *Anaphalis margaritacea*, with gray-green leaves and pearly white flowers in late summer. Its near relative, *Anaphalis triplinervis*, also grows in dry shade. For a taller and more dominant display, plant *Crambe cordifolia* (colewort), which grows 5–6ft/1.5–1.8m high. It has branching stems with white flowers in early summer. Epimediums grow about 12in/30cm high and will cover the soil with colorful leaves and flowers. *Persicaria affinis* (still better known as *Polygonum affine*) also makes good ground cover.

Plants for moist shade

Several shrubs flourish in moist soil and shade, including camellias, whose blooms herald the approach of spring, *Elaeagnus angustifolia*, *Gaultheria shallon*, *Gaultheria procumbens*, and *Fatsia japonica*, with its distinctively large, glossy green leaves. Herbaceous perennials include *Aruncus dioicus* (goatsbeard), *Brunnera macrophylla*, *Cimicifuga racemosa* (bugbane), the popular hostas, *Lysimachia nummularia* (creeping Jenny), *Pulmonaria angustifolia* (lungwort), and *Rodgersia pinnata*.

Climbers and shrubs for a shady wall

It is inevitable that one side of a wall will be in shade. Fortunately, there are climbers that grow well, even on the northern, less congenial side of a wall.

Garrya elliptica is an evergreen wall shrub that grows on both sunny and shady sides of walls, but it flowers best on the brighter side. *Hydrangea anomala petiolaris* (climbing hydrangea) is a vigorous climber that does well on a north or north-east wall. Its creamy white flowers appear during early summer. *Jasminum nudiflorum* (winter jasmine) also grows well on an almost sunless, north-facing wall, and produces yellow flowers during winter. Several pyracanthas with attractive berries will grow against both sunny and shady walls.

Shade-loving ferns

Most ferns grow in shade and damp soil although some will thrive in dry areas that are fully shaded. Visit a specialist nursery and you will find a wide range of plants that are easy to grow and make a very useful addition to the shaded border. Ferns that will grow in moisture-retentive soil include *Asplenium scolopendrium* (hart's-tongue fern) (also known as *Phyllitis scolopendrium* or *Scolopendrium vulgare*), *Matteuccia struthiopteris* (ostrich fern), *Onoclea sensibilis* (sensitive fern), and *Osmunda regalis* (royal fern). Ferns suitable for dry soil, as well as modestly moist soil, include the widely grown *Dryopteris filix-mas* (male fern), *Athyrium filix-femina* (lady fern), and *Polypodium vulgare* (the wall polypody).

GROUND-COVER PLANTS IN SHADE

There are many suitable plants, but first take the opportunity to improve the soil (see previous page). Plants include:

- *Ajuga reptans* (bugleweed)
- *Alchemilla mollis* (lady's mantle)
- *Bergenia* (elephant's ears)
- *Epimedium* (barrenwort)
- *Hedera* (ivy)
- *Hypericum calycinum* (rose of Sharon)
- *Lamium maculatum* (dead nettle)
- *Pachysandra terminalis*
- *Tellima grandiflora*
- *Tiarella cordifolia*
- *Vinca* (periwinkle)

▼ *Many ferns thrive in shade and moist soil, although some do well in dry soil. Here is a superb example of a fern with* Fatsia japonica.

creating lawns from seed

In temperate regions there are two main ways to create lawns: sowing seed or laying turfs. There are other methods, however. In warm climates, dibbling tufts of grass about 3in/7.5cm apart is successful. In a tropical climate, spreading a mud plaster of chopped grass, water, and soil works well.

Preparing the site

Whether you create a lawn from seed or by laying turfs, preparation of the soil is the same. First, check that the ground is well drained and, if necessary, install drains. In winter, dig the soil, removing perennial weeds. A few weeks before sowing seeds, rake the area level or with a slight slope. Firm the soil by shuffling sideways over the whole area, so that it is uniformly firm. Do not use a roller. Rake the soil to create a fine tilth.

Sowing lawn seed

About a week before sowing lawn seed (usually in late spring, or from late summer to early fall), scatter a general fertilizer evenly over the area at 1½oz per sq yd/50g per sq m. Use a metal rake to mix it lightly into the surface. Wait for a day when the surface soil is dry, and use string to section the area into strips 3½ft/1m wide. Then use a couple of bamboo canes 4ft/1.2m long to form a 3½ft/1m square at one end of the strip.

Into this area sow lawn seed at the rate of 1½oz per sq yd/50g per sq m. Sowing less than this amount results in a thin, sparse lawn, while too much produces masses of tightly bunched seedlings susceptible to disease.

Next, move one of the canes to form another square and sow with more seed, continuing in this way until the whole area has been covered. Then, standing on a plank of wood, rake the seed lightly and evenly into the surface. It is important that you do not walk on newly sown areas of lawn because this depresses the soil and seed may stick to your shoes. If the weather forecast indicates a dry period, water the soil lightly but thoroughly. Also provide protection from hungry birds by stretching black thread about 6in/15cm above the surface and 6in/20cm apart. An alternative method which is unlikely to harm birds is to lay large sheets of black polyethylene on the sown surface to give protection and retain moisture. However, the sheets must be removed immediately once the grass seeds have germinated.

▶ *Lawns provide a natural foil that shows off plants to perfection. Grass paths may also be sown to connect parts of a garden.*

ADVANTAGES OF SOWING SEEDS

- Cheaper than laying turfs.
- Lighter work than laying turfs.
- Easier to create intricately shaped areas.
- There is lawn seed for almost every part of the garden, from sunny sites to shady areas, and from play areas to ornamental lawns.

DISADVANTAGES OF SOWING SEEDS

- It takes from 3–4 months before a lawn can be used.
- Cats often disturb the sown surface, and dogs and toddlers may tread on it.
- Perennial weeds can be a problem if the area has not been thoroughly prepared.

HINTS AND TIPS

Always buy a little more seed than you will need. Small bare areas often occur and it is useful to have the same type and batch of seed handy to re-sow them.

lawns from seed

1 Level the soil and remove any large stones. Work in a general fertilizer at 1½ oz per sq yd/50g per sq m using a garden rake or metal-tined lawn rake.

2 Stretch two garden lines across the area to be sown, a yard apart. Then, place two garden canes 4ft/1.2m long to form a square yard.

3 Scatter seed evenly into each square at the rate of 1½ oz per sq yd/50g per sq m. Take care to sow each part of the square, not just the center.

4 When the square has been sown, move one of the canes to form another square. Then repeat the sowing until the row is complete. Use a garden or lawn rake to work the seed lightly into the surface.

47

creating lawns from turfs

Lawns made of turfs are thought to be instant features, but be warned, you will have to wait at least four weeks before they are established and can be used. Soil preparation is exactly the same as when creating lawns from seed (pages 46–47).

Laying turfs

Turfs can be laid from spring to fall, although early fall is the most popular period because the soil is warm and usually moist. After preparing the soil thoroughly, use a metal rake to level the surface and, about one week before laying turfs, scatter a general fertilizer at 2oz per sq yd/70g per sq m. Rake it lightly into the surface.

Mark out the area to be laid and stretch a garden line down one edge. As an insurance against dry weather and damage to the edges, make the area about 3in/7.5cm wider than required. Should the edges become dry the lawn will not be spoiled because it can be cut back to the desired size.

Start laying the lawn by positioning a row of turfs along the garden line, closely abutting their ends. Then, place a plank of wood 8in/20cm wide and 8–10ft/2.4–3m long on top of the turfs. Stand on this plank (moving it as necessary) to lay another row of turfs. Stagger the joints. Again, move the plank and lay another row, continuing until the whole area is covered.

Always insure that each turf is in close contact with the soil by using a firming device made from a thick piece of wood, 1–1½ft/45cm square, attached at its center to a vertical handle, usually a thick, 5ft/1.5m-long pole. Gaps will inevitably occur between the turfs, at their ends and their sides. Trickle a mixture of equal parts of sieved soil and peat substitute into the gaps. When the area has been turfed, use a sprinkler.

Types of turf

Two main types of turf are used to make garden lawns. One is meadow turf cut 3ft/90cm long, 12in/30cm wide, and 1½in/36mm thick; but expect variations. It comes from pasture and is usually the cheapest way to buy turfs.

Cultivated turf is the other type and is sometimes known as seeded turf. It is grown especially for sale, costs more than meadow turf, and is sold in rolls, but check the exact size because it can vary.

ADVANTAGES OF LAYING TURFS

⚘ A usable surface is usually created about four weeks after laying.
⚘ Eliminates problems with birds, cats, and dogs.
⚘ Ideal for families with young children.
⚘ Turfs can be laid from spring to fall, but not when the soil is dry. If it becomes dry, regular watering is essential.

DISADVANTAGES OF LAYING TURFS

⚘ More expensive than sowing seeds.
⚘ Much heavier work than sowing seeds.
⚘ Turfs have to be laid within 24 hours of delivery. If left rolled up, the grass becomes yellow and the edges begin to dry. If laying is delayed, be prepared to unroll the turfs and water them.

HINTS AND TIPS

Always buy a few more turfs than you need. This is important where the sides of a lawn are curved. Also note that because turfs are laid in a staggered pattern there is always some wastage at the ends.

laying turfs

1 Prepare the soil thoroughly and rake in a general fertilizer. Stretch a garden line along one side of the planned lawn and lay a turf alongside it. Lay other turfs, with their ends butted against each other.

2 Put a wide, strong plank on top of the laid turf and stand on it to lay a another line, closely abutting the first row and with the end joints staggered. Never stand on the turf because it causes indentations.

3 Improvise a firmer by tapping on a plank of wood with the heel of a hammer, or fashion one from a thick piece of wood 18in/45cm square, with a vertical pole 5ft/1.5m long, fixed at its center.

4 Trickle a mixture of sieved soil and peat substitute into the joints and use a broom or besom to work it into the cracks. When the lawn is complete, use a sprinkler to soak the lawn area gently but thoroughly.

▲ A well-maintained lawn creates a sense of space and highlights plants and other ornamental garden features.

chamomile lawns, thyme paths

These lawns and paths are unusual and colorful features that can be fitted into most gardens, whatever their size. Chamomile lawns have a long history and were popular in Elizabethan England, when bowls were played on their scented surface. The aroma of thyme adds a dimension to a garden walk.

Chamomile lawns

These lawns are planted with *Chamaemelum nobile*, formerly and widely known as *Anthemis nobilis*, a prostrate, mat-forming herbaceous perennial with finely dissected leaves that release a fruity scent when bruised and walked on. The non-flowering variety, 'Treneague' has a scent rather like bananas.

Weeds can be a problem in new chamomile lawns and thorough preparation is necessary. Dig the area 12in/30cm deep in winter and remove all perennial weeds. Leave for 12 months, pulling or digging up weeds as they appear. In the second winter, dig the soil again, and plant in the spring.

Planting a chamomile lawn

Rake the area level and shuffle sideways over the surface to firm it evenly. Then, rake again to remove footprints. If the lawn is dry, water the soil thoroughly and wait until the surface is dry and crumbly before planting.

You can plant the lawn in late spring or early summer. Space the plants 6–8in/15–20cm apart in staggered rows, and use a trowel to make holes that do not constrict the roots of each plant. Check that the crown of each plant is just below the surface, then firm the soil and water the whole lawn lightly but thoroughly. When the plants start to grow into a lawn, trim them with sharp hedging shears.

Thyme paths

Use *Thymus serpyllum* (English or wild thyme) to form a colorful, scented path. It is evergreen and carpet-forming, with richly fragrant gray-green leaves. It bears flowers ranging from white to pink to red, and flowers through much of the summer. When established, thyme has a 18–24in/45–60cm spread, but in order to achieve rapid cover set the plants closer together.

Creating a thyme path

During winter, mark the width of the path and dig the area thoroughly to remove perennial weeds. Leave the surface rough so that the weather will break down the surface to a fine tilth. In spring, rake the soil and place stepping stones on the surface (check that the spacing is right for everyone who will use the path). Set the stepping stones into the ground so the surface of each stone is about ½in/12mm above the soil surface. To promote quick covering, set the plants 9–12in/23–30cm apart. Firm the soil around them and

water the whole lawn thoroughly. Until the path is established, water it regularly, especially at the edges where the soil tends to dry out.

▲ *Chamomile lawns, formed of finely dissected midgreen leaves with all the fruity fragrance of chamomile, always attract attention.*

▶ *Thyme paths become decorative ribbons of color throughout summer and are ideal for linking one part of a garden with another.*

SCENTED SEATS

These are an original feature in a small garden. They are raised, planted structures about 18in/45cm high, 4–6ft/1.2–1.8m long and 20–24in/50–60cm deep, planted with chamomile or thyme. Because the bed is raised the soil tends to become dry, especially if the weather is hot and sunny, and so regular and thorough watering is essential. A variation on this type of seat is to intersperse the plants with small paving slabs. As well as providing sitting positions the slabs help keep the soil moist and cool.

water gardens

Water introduces tranquillity and movement to a garden. Established garden ponds, perhaps nestling in an open, sunny corner of a garden, create a restful atmosphere, especially when covered with waterlilies, and with dragonflies hovering over the surface.

Water features for all gardens

It is quite possible to have a water feature in your garden without digging a pond, and in a garden to be used by young children, an alternative is often welcome. There may be a fountain splashing over pebbles, or water in a shallow trough being recirculated by a pump. Such a feature may be quite small and so there is often room for one on a patio.

A pond can be built to any desired shape or size. The water surface can be level with the surrounding ground or raised by about 18in/45cm. A pond at ground level with an informal outline can be merged with a bog garden or a wildlife area. Several decades ago, ponds were nearly always square or rectangular, and made of concrete. Building one was hard work, and unless it was reinforced it soon cracked. Modern bowl-shaped ponds with gently sloping sides are a popular choice and more durable.

Today, ponds are mainly formed using a flexible liner (also called a pond liner) or come as a rigid liner (called a preformed pond or a molded shell).

▲ *Garden ponds introduce tranquillity and peace into a garden. The range of plants is wide, from waterlilies to fragrant marginal plants.*

SELECTING FOUNTAINS

⚙ The spray should not fall on waterlilies or marginal plants.
⚙ The height of the spray should not be more than half the pond's width.
⚙ In windy areas, use fountains that produce large droplets of water.
⚙ Do not allow water droplets to disturb floating plants.

Flexible liners are used to line holes dug to the desired shape and depth. Their durability depends on the material used to make them. Polyethylene liners are low cost and have a relatively short life, especially when exposed to sunlight. Butyl rubber sheeting is the most durable, lasting for over 20 years, but it is also the most expensive.

Liners must be laid on an underlay to prevent the water pressure from puncturing them on sharp stones. Ready-made rigid liners are sunk into a hole. The cheapest type is made of plastic, which has the shortest lifespan. Glassfiber shells are more costly but will last for 20 years or more.

Choosing waterlilies

These plants need careful selection to insure that vigorous varieties do not dominate and overcrowd small ponds. Waterlilies are usually put into four classifications: dwarf; small; medium; and vigorous. Dwarf types suit ponds with a depth of 4–10in/10–25cm; small lilies need a 6–18in/15–45cm depth; the medium lilies need a depth of 1–2ft/30–60cm, and the vigorous type need a water depth of 1½–3ft/45–90cm.

To plant a waterlily (*Nymphaea spp*), put it in a plastic mesh container with compost and cover it with a layer of clean pea gravel 1in/2.5cm thick. Soak the compost and place the container in the pond. Using bricks as a stand for the container, position it so that the waterlily leaves float on the surface. Remove the bricks progressively as the plant grows, always keeping the leaves on the surface.

Miniponds on patios

Even a patio in the smallest garden can have a water feature. Stout wooden tubs are ideal summer homes for miniature waterlilies and other aquatic plants. They contain only a small volume of water, so unfortunately must be emptied or moved to a greenhouse or a conservatory during winter. First-rate miniature waterlilies include:

Nymphaea 'Aurora'—pinkish-yellow, then orange and later red.

Nymphaea 'Indiana'—orange, with orange-red stamens.

Nymphaea tetragona— white, with yellow stamens.

Marginal aquatics include:

Carex elata 'Aurea'— narrow, golden leaves.

Scirpus latifolia 'Zebrinus'—quill-like stems banded green and white.

▲ *A raised pond creates a distinctive feature on a patio. It needs to be built with materials that harmonize with other garden structures.*

FLEXIBLE LINER

Mark out the approximate position of the pond with string, then a garden hose to indicate the shape and size. Dig out the area, forming a shelf about 12in/30cm below the surface for the marginal plants. Check that the top and the shelf are level. Then use a spade to remove a strip about 10in/25cm wide and 2–3in/5–7.5cm deep from around the pool for the edging stones. Remove any stones from the surface and line the base with soft sand. Position the liner and weight its edges with paving temporarily. Fill the pond using a hose pipe, adjusting the weights so that the liner takes the shape of the hole. Trim the liner so that 6–8in/15–20cm can be folded back and edging stones cemented into position over the edges.

building a rock garden

Rock gardens make delightful features in small gardens, especially as a large number of small plants can be grown in them. A rock garden can be grown on a gentle slope and on a freestanding mound created from well-drained soil, with stones added in stratified rows.

Rock gardens

If you are fortunate enough to have a garden with a slope toward the south or west, a rock garden is easily created with pieces of natural stone such as limestone or sandstone positioned to resemble stratified rows. For a rock garden with an area of about 15sq yd/4.5sq m you will need between 1–2 tons of stone.

The range of plants for rock gardens is wide and includes alpines and small herbaceous perennials, dwarf bulbs, and miniature and slow-growing conifers. Dwarf shrubs such as *Cotoneaster linearifolius* grow about 12in/30cm high and 20in/50cm wide and give a permanent structure. There are many other shrubs including thyme, the

glorious yellow-flowered *Hypericum olympica*, and *Zauschneria californica* (Californian fuchsia) with red, tubular, fuchsia-like flowers during late summer and early fall.

Freestanding rock gardens

These have natural stone in stratified layers, like a rock garden on a slope. They often provide more space for plants than a rock garden built on a slope because it is possible to plant the front and the two sides. Since the front is usually small, do not dominate it with large, shrub-like plants but use miniature, columnar, and slow-growing conifers to create the impression of height. These include *Juniperus communis* 'Compressa'

STAR PLANTS

Aubrieta deltoidea	Sedum acre
Aurina saxatilis	Saponaria ocymoides

◀ *Rock gardens that are harmonized with a gently flowing stream are immediately more interesting than when on their own.*

(18in/45cm high after 10 years) and *Juniperus scopulorum* 'Skyrocket' (6ft/1.8m high after 10 years). Where interest is needed at the base of the rock garden to give the impression of extra width, plant *Juniperus squamata* 'Blue Star' (15in/38cm high and 24in/60cm, wide after 10 years) or *Juniperus × pfitzeriana* 'Gold Coast' (20in/50cm high and 30in/75cm wide after 10 years).

Dry-stone walls

These walls look wonderful when their sides are covered by colorful flowers. Several rock garden plants can achieve this effect, but perhaps none better than *Aurinia saxatilis*, better known as *Alyssum saxatile*. On a dry-stone wall it spreads 12–18in/30–45cm wide, and trails golden-yellow flowers more than 24in/60cm. There are several attractive varieties. *Aubrieta deltoidea* is an evergreen perennial that bears cross-shaped flowers in shades of rose-lilac to purple in spring and early summer.

Plants may also be grown along the top of the wall so their tumbling foliage softens the wall's sharp outline. Such plants include *Saponaria ocymoides*, with pale pink flowers through most of the summer that trail to about 2ft/60cm, and *Sedum acre* 'Aureum', which has bright yellow flowers and spreads to 2ft/60cm. Raised beds are similar to dry-stone walls, but with the wall encircling a bed 1½–3ft/45–90cm high up to 5ft/1.5m wide.

Scree beds

Scree beds are often placed around rock gardens. However, in very small gardens they are lovely on their own. Suitable plants range from miniature and slow-growing conifers to dwarf bulbs and perennials such as aethionema, erodium, *Phlox douglasii*, and silene.

▲ *Scree beds are ideal for small gardens and can be added to an existing rock garden or constructed as features on their own.*

MAKING A SCREE BED

A scree bed is very easy to construct. Mark out an area at the base of a rock garden, so that it widens out like a mushroom. Dig the area 15in/38cm deep and fill it with 6in/15cm of clean rubble. Over this spread a 2in/5cm layer of coarse sand. Mix a compost of one part top-soil, one of moist peat

 substitute and three of sharp grit and spread a 6in/15cm layer over the entire area. Position rocks as if they were a small outcrop from the main rock garden. Plant the alpines in the compost. Last, spread a 1in/2.5cm layer of gravel over the surface to reduce water loss.

bush and shrub roses

The range of large-flowered bush roses (hybrid teas) and cluster-flowered bush roses (floribundas) is wide, and each year more are introduced. The many species of rose with a dramatic and subtle range of colors extend the range, and the more recent New English Roses make the choice still harder.

Using roses

It was once thought that the only way to grow bush roses was in formal beds flanked by paths or lawns. Today, they are used in many other situations. Prostrate roses cover the soil, patio roses in pots decorate patios, species roses adorn shrub borders, and weeping standards rise from beds and lawns. Small rose bushes can be planted in rock gardens and also in window boxes. These include 'Baby Masquerade' (yellow to pink and red), 'Cinderella' (white, tinged with pink), 'Darling Flame' (orange-red, with yellow anthers), 'Black Jade' (deep red, almost black) and 'Popcorn' (white, honey-scented).

Weeping standards are well known for their beautiful, cascading outlines. They are produced by nurserymen budding a variety on a rootstock about 51in/130cm high. When mature, the head is 5–6ft/1.5–1.8m high, with stems cascading from the top. Rambler varieties are mainly used and include 'Albéric Barbier' (cream), 'Crimson Shower' (red), 'François Juranville' (salmon-pink) and 'Goldfinch' (yellow, fading to white).

Companion planting bush roses

Bush roses can be attractively grouped with other plants. Plant the buttercup-yellow floribunda 'Chinatown' in front of *Clematis* 'Countess of Lovelace', a large-flowered variety that will flourish sprawling over a fence or a garden wall. The clematis flowers through summer into the fall (double-flowered forms bloom during summer, and single forms in late summer and fall). Its deep lavender flowers look handsome beside those of the yellow rose. Underplant white-flowering bush roses with the evergreen perennial *Tiarella cordifolia* (foam flower), which has a low mound of maple-shaped leaves and creamy white flowers in late spring and early summer.

▲ Rosa gallica officinalis, *(apothecary's rose or red rose of Lancaster) bears large, loosely-formed, semidouble, rose-crimson flowers.*

The popular floribunda 'Queen Elizabeth' has cyclamen-pink flowers that look superb highlighted against yew. Plant the large-flowered yellow 'Grandpa Dickson' against the dark purple leaves of the deciduous shrub *Berberis thunbergii* 'Atropurpurea'. And, for additional color, plant the half-hardy annual *Nicotiana* 'Lime Green' in front of them.

Companion planting shrub roses

The range of shrub roses is wide and many are old roses. They range from Albas to Moss roses, and form attractive combinations with other plants. The Alba 'Königin von Danemark' has deep pink flowers that look striking against the silvery leaved, weeping tree *Pyrus salicifolia* 'Pendula'. A splendid collaboration is the modern shrub rose 'Nevada' with creamy white flowers, and blue delphiniums and campanulas. The 'New' English Rose 'Constance Spry' has pink flowers best highlighted by a cluster of silver-leaved plants.

▲ *Roses make distinctive backgrounds for low border plants and often enrich the air around garden benches with rich fragrance.*

▼ *Many shrub roses have an informal habit and can be allowed to cascade and spread across paths and over lawn edges.*

PATIO ROSES

This is a relatively new group of roses, coming between miniature roses and small floribundas. They are sometimes called dwarf cluster-flowered bush roses and are ideal on a patio. Even when you are sitting down they do not obstruct the view. Most are between 1½ft/45cm and 2ft/60cm high, and include 'Anna Ford' (vivid orange-red), 'Living Easy' (apricot orange blend), 'Betty Boop' (yellow ivory, edged red), 'Robin Redbreast' (red, with a pale center) and 'Top Marks' (bright, vivid orange-vermilion).

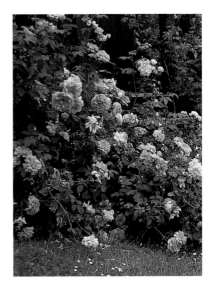

climbing and rambler roses

Climbers and ramblers look dramatic in any garden and are still more spectacular when the color complements its background. A white wall makes a perfect backcloth for roses with yellow or scarlet flowers, whereas a gray stone wall is better for those with pink or red flowers.

Climber or rambler?

Climbing and rambling roses produce attractive flowers, but each is distinctive in several ways. Climbers have a more permanent framework than ramblers and their flowers, when compared with those of ramblers, are larger and borne singly or in small clusters. Rambling roses have long, flexible stems that sometimes grow 3–3.6m/10–12ft in length in one season and bear flowers in large trusses, usually only once a year.

Covering trees

Old, perhaps slightly unsightly trees can be transformed by training climbers to scramble up through their branches. Plant them several feet to one side of the trunk, and replace the soil with a mixture of topsoil and well-rotted garden compost or manure. Firm the soil, plant the rose, water the soil, and use a stout stake to guide the stems to the tree trunk.

Suitable varieties range in vigor, and can be selected to suit the tree that needs brightening. Roses to consider include 'Rambling Rector' (9ft/2.7m, rambler, creamy white), 'Emily Gray' (15ft/4.5m, rambler, butter-yellow); 'Mme Grégoire

Staechelin' (climber, 20ft/6m, rosy carmine-pink), 'Paul's Himalayan Musk' (rambler, 30ft/9m, blush-pink), 'Sympathie' (climber, 15ft/4.5m, blood-red), and 'Wedding Day' (rambler, 25ft/7.5m, creamy white to blush).

Pillar roses

These contribute interest in small gardens. All you need is a rustic pole 8–10ft/2.4–3m high or a tripod made of rough-cut lumber. In quite a small area, several pillars can be inexpensively

◀ *Pergolas and free-standing trellis provide support for many roses. They can be positioned alongside paths and the edges of lawns.*

GROUND-COVER ROSES

Ground-smothering roses do not actually form a weed-suppressing blanket of stems, leaves and flowers, but a low mass of color. Choices include 'Baby Blanket' (pink), 'Nozomi' (pearly-pink to white), 'Pheasant' (pink), 'Rosy Cushion' (pink), and 'Snow Carpet' (white). The County Series includes 'Avon' (pearly white), 'Essex' (rich reddish-pink), 'Hertfordshire' (carmine-pink), and 'Wiltshire' (pink).

constructed. Climbers with moderate vigor are best for clothing such structures and include 'Bantry Bay' (semidouble, deep pink), 'Compassion' (salmon-pink, tinted apricot-orange), 'Handel' (creamy, edged pink-red), 'Pink Perpetue' (bright rose-pink), and 'Reine Victoria' (shell-pink).

Climbers for cold walls

A cold wall is not the best place to grow roses, but a few sturdy ramblers and climbers will survive such conditions and produce acceptable displays. Hardy and vigorous varieties to consider include

'Albéric Barbier' (rambler, cream), 'Félicité et Perpétue' (rambler, white), 'Morning Jewel' (climber, bright pink), 'New Dawn' (climber, pink blush), and 'Zéphirine Drouhin' (climber, deep pink).

Companion planting climbers and ramblers

In the same way that bush roses can be planted in attractive arrangements with other plants, so can climbers and ramblers. For example, the rambler 'Bobbie James', which is often grown over pergolas and clambering up trees, has large clusters of semidouble, creamy

white flowers that look attractive combined with the lavender-blue flowers of *Nepeta* × *faassenii* (catmint), a bushy perennial growing about 18in/45cm high. It flowers throughout summer. Another good combination is the modern climber 'New Dawn', with semidouble, blush-pink flowers with the vigorous hybrid *Clematis* 'Perle d'Azure' with light pink flowers. It flowers from early to late summer.

▼ *Rose 'Helen Knight', a distinctive climber, creates a mass of small, buttercup-yellow flowers in late spring and early summer.*

cottage gardens

Few gardening styles have such a relaxed and informal atmosphere as a cottage garden. It is rich in nostalgia, and packed with flowers, fruits, vegetables, and herbs. Such informality can easily be created in small gardens, with arbors and trellises providing secluded areas.

Screening plants

Few climbers compare with the scrambling *Clematis vitalba* (old man's beard), widely seen in English hedgerows. It is usually remembered for its glistening, silky seed heads in fall, which often continue into winter. Elizabethans praised it for covering hedges, but in a small cottage garden it is too vigorous and there are other clematis with more attractive and delicate flowers. They include *Clematis macropetala, C. flammula,* and *C. orientalis. C. montana* is also attractive but often too large for small areas. Honeysuckle is also an excellent cottage garden climber, best given rustic supports. And as well as being grown for food, pole beans can be used as screening plants; try them clambering up a 6ft/1.8m-high tripod. Cordon and espalier apples also make useful screens. Where possible, plant some of the older varieties with superb flavors and textures. Try 'Rome', a cooking apple, and for eating, 'Esopus Spuitzenberg', 'Gravenstein', 'Arkansas Black' and 'Northern spy' to bring back flavors that were common in the past.

Flower borders

Aim for a medley of shrubs, trees, herbaceous perennials, bulbs, and annuals planted or sown in attractive groups, each plant complementing its neighbors. From spring to fall memorable plant associations can be created.

❀ Spring—tulips offer a wide range of colors. For a mixture of yellow, orange-red, and blue try a deep-blue forget-me-not and a combination of orange-red and yellow tulips. If you prefer a medley of blue, scarlet, and gold flowers, plant pale blue forget-me-nots and the scarlet and gold single early tulip 'Keizerskroon'. Alternatively, for a white and blue display, plant a carpet of the biennial *Bellis perennis* (common daisy) with violet-blue Parrot tulips. These arrangements are ideal for beds and under windows. For a larger spring display in a prominent border plant the yellow-flowered deciduous shrub *Forsythia* 'Lynwood' with small groups of red-flowered Kaufmanniana tulips.

▲ *The large, brilliantly colored flowers of Papaver orientale (oriental poppy) make a dramatic display during early summer.*

STAR PLANTS

Clematis montana	*Hydrangea macrophylla*
Geranium endressii	*Sedum* 'Herbstfreude'

❀ Summer—*Lilium candidum* (madonna lily) has pure white flowers, and is a suitable companion for foxgloves, which have tall stems bearing bell-shaped flowers in a color range from purple, to pink to red. Plant the scrambling *Clematis flammula*, with small, sweetly-scented flowers, and *Aconitum napellus* (monkshood) with its deep blue, helmet-shaped flowers, for an unusual combination of climbers with perennials.

Roses are also superb in summer displays. 'Buff Beauty' bears warm, apricot-yellow flowers that form a pleasing partnership with the lavender-blue *Nepeta* × *faassenii* (catmint) and *Papaver orientale* 'Perry's White' (oriental poppy). Another good combination involves the damask rose 'Mme Hardy',

with white flowers, and pink varieties of *Geranium endressii*. The bourbon rose 'Mme Isaac Pereire' is bushy and shrubby, with crimson flowers that harmonize with tulips, lilies, peonies, and lilacs.

❀ Fall—for a large display, plant blue varieties of the hardy, deciduous dome-shaped shrub *Hydrangea macrophylla* in front of the evergreen shrubby *Eucryphia* × *nymansensis*, which produces cream flowers.

Another attractive duo for the fall is the evergreen border plant *Sedum* 'Herbstfreude' and the bulbous *Colchicum* 'Waterlily'. The *Sedum* is well known for the display created by its richly colored fall flowers, which eventually become orange-brown.

▲ A combination of tulips and fragrant forget-me-nots (myosotis) never fails to capture attention in spring and early summer.

▼ Border geraniums produce magnificent displays throughout summer. There are many varieties and colors.

scented gardens

Scented flowers and aromatic leaves can enrich the air with many different fragrances. The range of scents is amazingly wide, and even in temperate regions there is a choice of over 100 fragrances. They include scents from chocolate and pineapple to banana and lemon.

Siting fragrant plants

The perfect site for a perfumed garden is sheltered from strong winds, which disperse scents, free from frosts, which limit the growing period of tender plants, and slopes gently toward the sun, to capture the warmth that encourages plants to emit their fragrances. Few gardens have all these qualities, but garden areas suitable for perfumed plants can be made by planting hedges, erecting freestanding trellis, and introducing tender plants in frost-free areas.

Flower borders

Many herbaceous perennials emit delicious scents, notably the short-lived, hardy *Hesperis matronalis* (sweet rocket). Its white, mauve, or purple flowers appear in early to midsummer to drench borders with their sweet fragrance, especially in the evening. *Saponaria officinalis* (soapwort) also emits a sweet scent from its single, pink, salver-shaped flowers which appear in mid- to late summer. *Phlox paniculata* has strongly perfumed flowers from mid- to late summer, and is perhaps better known. There are many varieties in colors from white to pink and red.

Establish summer color with rich fragrance in your garden quickly by planting a mix of *Matthiola bicornis* (night-scented stock), which bears pink to mauve flowers during mid- and late summer, and *Malcolmia maritima* (Virginia stock). Sow the seeds in friable soil beneath windows, and in successive sowings from spring to midsummer.

Once a favorite of the French Empress Josephine Bonaparte, *Reseda odorata* (mignonette) is a cottage-garden hardy annual with clusters of small, white and yellow richly scented flowers through the summer. It can be grown in window boxes and in pots on balconies.

◀ *This pairing of English lavender (Lavandula angustifolia) and rue (Ruta graveolens) brings scent and color to small gardens.*

AROMATIC-LEAVED SHRUBS

Caryopteris x *clandonensis*—pungent

Choisya ternata (Mexican orange blossom)

Lavandula angustifolia (lavender)—lavender

Rosmarinus officinalis (rosemary)—rosemary

Ruta graveolens (rue)—pungent and acrid

It is said that success and good fortune will attend a lover who rolls in a bed of mignonette.

There are several diminutive bulbs which will bring color and perfume to a rock garden and along the edges of paths. *Galanthus nivalis* (common snowdrop) and *Iris reticulata* both have violet-scented flowers during late winter and early spring.

Trees and shrubs

Many trees and shrubs are sweetly perfumed, and some have an unexpected fragrance. *Prunus padus* 'Wateri' (bird cherry) is a deciduous tree with a spreading habit. It bears drooping tassels of white flowers which are almond-scented in early summer. *Prunus × yedoensis* (Potomac cherry) is also almond-scented. For a cowslip fragrance plant the deciduous shrub *Corylopsis pauciflora*, with pale primrose yellow flowers in mid- and late spring. *Helichrysum serotinum* is known as the

curry plant because it is redolent of curry spices.

For honey fragrance, plant the informal *Ulex europaeus* 'Flore Pleno' (double-flowered gorse). The deciduous philadelphus shrubs have flowers with an orange-blossom aroma that will pervade the garden in midsummer. *Cytisus battandieri* (pineapple broom) bears pineapple-scented, golden-yellow flowers if planted against a south-facing wall, and the deciduous tree *Malus* 'Brandywine' has abundant pink flowers.

STAR PLANTS

Galanthus nivalis

Helichrysum serotinum

Hesperis matronalis

Phlox paniculata

Ulex europaeus 'Flore Pleno'

▼ Few scented cottage garden plants are as attractive as **Hesperis** matronalis *(sweet rocket), with a rich scent in the evening.*

ground-cover plants

Plants that smother soil with foliage prevent the growth of weeds and are welcome in any garden. The choice is wide and includes herbaceous perennials, shrubs, and a few climbers such as large-leaved ivies like Hedera colchica 'Sulphur Heart'.

Border perennials

Most border perennials are herbaceous but some do retain their foliage through winter. Most prefer full sun or light shade, but others will grow out of the sun.
☸ Sun or shade—although some plants can grow in either light or shade, do not expect the same display in both. Most plants when given plenty of light and moisture will flower better than those in shade with little moisture. The range of plants you need includes *Alchemilla mollis* (lady's mantle) with lime-green, hairy leaves, and yellow-green, star-shaped flowers. Bergenias, with their large, elephant-like leaves, also flower in spring. Epimediums are daintier and cover the ground with heart-shaped leaves that assume attractive tints in the fall and through much of winter. *Geranium grandiflorum* is herbaceous, with a spreading habit and blue-purple flowers in early and midsummer. And *Hemerocallis* (day lily) forms large clumps, with arching, strap-like leaves and lily-like flowers. Avoid heavy shade because this reduces its ability to flower.
Persicaria affinis forms mats of lance-shaped leaves and poker-like flower heads during mid- and late summer. *Saxifraga urbium* (London pride) has a more diminutive nature, with rosettes of leaves that carpet the soil and masses of pink, star-shaped flowers during late spring and early summer. *Lamium galeobdolon* 'Florentinum' (better known as *Lamium galeobdolon* 'Variegatum') is vigorous and spreading, with silver-flushed evergreen leaves that display bronze tints in winter. These plants will not thrive in dark shade.

◄ *Smothering the ground with plants looks attractive as well as making gardening easier by eliminating the need to pull up weeds.*

Lysimachia nummularia (creeping Jenny) has sprawling stems of rounded leaves and bright yellow, cup-shaped flowers during early and midsummer.

❁ Partial shade—the popular *Ajuga reptans* 'Multicolor' (bugle) has purple leaves, while *Brunnera macrophylla* has heart-shaped foliage and sprays of blue flowers in late spring and early summer; it dislikes dry soil. The range of hostas is wide and, with their often large leaves, they soon cloak the soil. *Pulmonaria angustifolia* (with the evocative name blue cowslip) has lance-shaped leaves and funnel-shaped, blue flowers in spring. *Pulmonaria saccharata* has leaves spotted silver-white. *Symphytum ibericum* spreads rapidly, with tubular, white flowers during spring, while *Tiarella cordifolia* (foam flower) is less dominant, with maple-like, light green leaves.

❁ Full sun—in strong sun, plant *Nepeta* × *faassenii* (catmint). It covers the soil with gray-green leaves and lavender-blue flowers from spring to fall. The wooly leaved *Stachys byzantina* (lamb's ears) never fails to attract attention.

Ground-covering shrubs

Many evergreen shrubs with a sprawling or bushy habit are ideal for covering soil with leaves and, sometimes, flowers.

STAR PLANTS

Alchemilla mollis
Hedera colchica 'Sulphur Heart'
Stachys byzantina

Hypericum calycinum (rose of Sharon) is a robust, ground-smothering plant that establishes itself quickly and even covers large banks. Throughout summer it bears golden-yellow flowers. Vincas also smother soil, but are best kept out of mixed lower beds because they are invasive. However, variegated forms are less invasive than all-green types. *Calluna* (heather) and *Erica* (heath) soon cover the ground with attractive leaves and flowers. Like *Gaultheria procumbens* (checkerberry), heathers and ericas need an acid soil. There are many others, including *Pachysandra terminalis*, with deep green leaves.

▼ *Where a large, flat area is planted with ground-covering plants, position large stepping stones to make access and maintenance easier.*

ornamental hedges

Creating hedges is more than just forming a boundary or screen. They can be gloriously rich in scents, have colorful berries, color contrasts within the same hedge, and harmonize or constrast with nearby plants. Even the ubiquitous privet can be attractive.

Hedge duos

To grow an unusual privet hedge, set two plants of *Ligustrum ovalifolium* 'Aureum' to one of *L. ovalifolium* along a row. This ratio produces a decorative, rather formal hedge, and will not allow the more vigorous all-green hedging to smother

the yellow. The hedge should be clipped regularly in order to keep it in shape. Planting variegated holly and yew to produce an attractive evergreen hedge which will grow very slowly. Set the plants in the ground alternately, about 4ft/1.2m apart.

Fragrant hedging

There is an astonishing range of hedging plants with fragrant flowers or leaves. The scents they emit include apple and raspberry. Several conifers used for hedging give off an unusual fragrance when their leaves are bruised.

For an apple-like scent plant *Thuja occidentalis* 'Smaragd'. Its dark-green foliage makes a dramatic backdrop for other plants. If a lemon fragrance delights you, choose *Cupressus macrocarpa* 'Goldcrest'. It has soft yellow foliage which, with age, becomes light green. The pineapple-scented *Thuja plicata* (western red cedar) has scaly, shiny, rich green foliage with white marks underneath. It is best reserved for a large boundary hedge. A fusion of resin and parsley is the smell given by *Chamaecyparis lawsoniana* 'Allumii', with soft blue-gray foliage, and *Chamaecyparis lawsoniana* 'Fletcheri' with feathery, blue-green leaves.

◀ *The evergreen shrub* Berberis darwinii *has masses of rich orange flowers in spring, followed by blue berries.*

Roses used for hedging offer more unusual scents, none better than 'Zephirine Drouhin' with raspberry-scented, vivid pink flowers. 'Penelope' has musk-scented, pale pink, semidouble flowers that fade slightly as they age. Several roses used for hedging have a sweet fragrance, including *Rosa rugosa* 'Roseraie de l'Hay' with crimson-purple flowers, 'Felicia' with salmon-pink flowers, and 'Prosperity' with creamy white blooms.

Two evergreen shrubs with memorable scents include *Lavandula angustifolia* 'Hidcote', with deep purple flowers 2in/5cm long and silver-green leaves. *Rosmarinus officinalis* (rosemary) also makes a lovely informal hedge.

Harmonies and contrasts

Color-themed herbaceous borders were traditionally backed by hedges that harmonized or contrasted with them. For example, the dark green leaves of yew highlight white, orange, blue, and green borders, while golden-variegated holly harmonizes with golden borders. *Tamarisk* (tamarix) was frequently used as a backcloth for a gray border. The deciduous *Fagus sylvatica* (beech), with young leaves that darken from bright green in spring to mid-green in summer, can be a striking backdrop for herbaceous plants. In the fall the hedge has the bonus of leaves that take on yellow and russet tints, competing for attention with end of season flower colors and seed heads.

▼ *Many roses can be used to form floriferous screens. They bring the atmosphere of a cottage garden to an urban plot.*

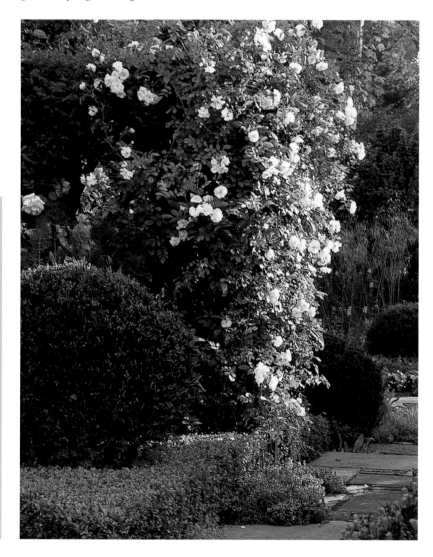

BERRIED DELIGHTS

Several shrubs used to make informal hedges also have attractive berries. These include:

• *Berberis darwinii*—evergreen, holly-like leaves and clusters of rich orange flowers in spring, followed by blue berries.

• *Berberis* × *stenophylla*—evergreen, with golden-yellow flowers in spring, followed by a peppering of globular, purple berries with a white bloom.

• *Hippophae rhamnoides* (sea buckthorn)—deciduous, with thick clusters of orange berries during fall and early winter.

• *Rosa rugosa* 'Roseraie de l'Hay'—deciduous, with crimson-purple flowers, followed by large, round, orange-red hips in early fall.

using plants in
small gardens

The range of plants, from flowers to vegetables and fruits, is wide and many have a reserved nature that makes them ideal for growing in small gardens. Several rootstocks for apples and pears have a dwarf nature and therefore are ideal for small areas, while growing peaches and nectarines against walls saves space. But it is flowers that create the most impact in a garden and borders and beds rich in a kaleidoscope of color are irresistible.

pink and red garden schemes

Red is a dramatic, fiery, dominant color in a garden, especially when used en masse in full sun, while pink is a desaturated red with a warmer feel. The perception of red changes through the day. In strong light it is bright, but as evening approaches it assumes darker shades until it turns almost black.

Flower borders

There is a wide choice of red and pink flowers for herbaceous borders and flowering bedding displays that will carry the color scheme through from early spring into fall. In herbaceous borders the plants range from tuberous-rooted alstroemerias, through the red and pink forms of the late-flowering *Aster novi-belgii* (Michaelmass daisy) and *Aster novae-angliae* (New England aster), to the dramatic red flowers of *Schizostylis coccinea* 'Major', which is aptly called the crimson flag. Many dahlias, from the smaller ball varieties to giant decoratives with flowers 10in/25cm wide, have lovely red flowers and will provide strong accents of color in late summer.

Spring flowering displays using bulbs and biennials, planted in late summer or early fall, add plenty of color. For a red and blue display, perhaps at the top of a drystone wall, you could plant a blue-flowered form of *Aubrieta deltoidea* adding colorful 'Madame Lefeber' tulips below. Summer displays, mainly of seed-raised plants, also add red and pink flowers, but none so arresting as *Begonia semperflorens* 'Cocktail Series' and *Salvia splendens* (scarlet sage).

BACKGROUND HARMONIES AND CONTRASTS

Many plants, from wall shrubs to ephemeral types in window boxes, wall baskets, and hanging baskets, look even better against the right background. Red and scarlet flowers are dramatically highlighted against white walls, while red and pink flowers harmonize with a gray stone wall.

◀ *Pink and red are romantic colors that give warm tones to a border. Pink flowers remain visible in the diminishing light of evening.*

Trees and shrubs

These produce massed displays and distinctive individual flowers. The spring-flowering deciduous azaleas, often in demure shades of red and pink, are a sure sign that gardens are bursting into life. A wild garden, with a high and light canopy of leaves, provides the right setting. Many have the bonus of richly colored leaves in the fall.

Other shrubs with pink or red flowers include the magnificent *Hibiscus syriacus* and *Kolkwitzia amabilis*, aptly known as the beauty bush for its pink, foxglove-like flowers with yellow throats. More dramatic and distinctive are the flowers of the deciduous, spring and early summer flowering *Magnolia liliiflora* 'Nigra'. Its flowers are upright, 3in/7.5cm long and deep reddish-purple. Offering a totally different style, the deciduous shrub *Leycesteria formosa* (Himalayan honeysuckle) has pendulous flowers formed of small, white flowers surrounded by highly conspicuous dark-claret bracts. It has the bonus of purplish-red berries in the fall.

Climbers and wall shrubs

This excellent range includes climbing and rambling roses, clematis and the rhizomatous-rooted *Tropaeolum speciosum* (Scottish flame flower) which dies down to soil level in the fall. From midsummer to fall it produces scarlet, trumpet-like flowers on long stems and loves to clamber through shrubs. Several large-flowered clematis have red or pink flowers including the popular 'Nelly Moser' in which each pale mauve-pink petal has a soft crimson stripe. 'Ville de Lyon' is bright carmine-red and 'Ernest Markham' is vivid magenta with a velvet sheen.

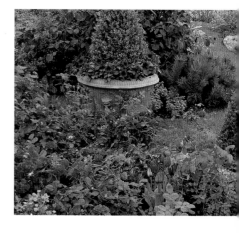

▲ *Many quite different plants create attractive combinations. Here a rose and a variety of slow-growing conifers form a pleasing group.*

▼ *Low beds, perhaps at the edge of a rock garden and mainly planted with pink and red plants, create a feature that radiates warmth.*

Key to planting

1 *Myosotis* (forget-me-not)

2 *Primula* 'Wanda'

3 *Candelabra primulas*

4 *Anemone × fulgens*

5 *Magnolia liliiflora*

6 Rhododendrons

7 Azaleas

8 *Aubrieta deltoidea* (aubrieta)

blue and purple borders

Blue is a calm color and when used in a garden will provide an atmosphere of tranquillity. Blue color schemes are thought to reduce blood pressure and slow up respiration and pulse rates. Enhance the color by adding patches of dull white and pale-lemon flowers, but not strong yellows.

Flower borders

Blue-flowered herbaceous borders usually come to life at the start of summer, when suddenly they abound in color. Perhaps no herbaceous perennial is more noticeable than *Delphinium elatum*. The large-flowered or elatum types have stiffly erect stems tightly packed with florets during early and midsummer, while the Belladonna forms are smaller, gracefully branched, and superb in cottage gardens. Within each type there is a wide range of colors.

Several perennial asters are blue, including *Aster amellus* (Italian aster) with large, daisy-like flowers with yellow centers. 'King George' is especially attractive, with soft blue-violet flowers. *Aster* × *frikartii* 'Mönch' is slightly less dramatic, with lavender-blue flowers. Again, the flowers have golden centers. Other blue-flowered herbaceous plants include *Echinacea purpurea* (purple coneflower) with purple-crimson, daisy-like flowers and distinctive large central cones, *Physostegia virginiana* (obedient plant) with spires of pink-mauve flowers, and *Tradescantia* × *andersoniana* 'Isis' which bears three-petaled, purple-blue flowers.

Several spring-flowering bulbs have blue flowers and include *Hyacinthus orientalis* (common hyacinth) and *Muscari armeniacum* (grape hyacinth), which is an ideal companion for polyanthus. *Myosotis alpestris* (forget-me-not) is a hardy perennial invariably grown as a biennial for its small and fragrant, azure-blue flowers borne in large clusters. There are many varieties and most will happily increase by self-seeding.

Summer-flowering bedding plants include blue-flowered forms of *Ageratum houstonianum*, such as 'Blue Danube' with masses of lavender-blue flowers, and *Lobelia erinus* with varieties such as 'Blue Moon' and 'Cambridge Blue'. There are also several trailing forms that are ideal for planting in window boxes and in hanging baskets.

▲ *Blue flowers create a contemplative and restful garden, while purple is more dramatic and looks best used in smaller groups.*

BACKGROUND HARMONIES AND CONTRASTS

Blue is a restful color that is at risk from being dominated by strong colors, but here are a few good combinations to try. Position plants with deep-blue or deep-purple flowers against gray stone walls. Soft blue flowers in large clusters harmonize with red brick walls.

Key to planting

❶ *Aster amellus*

❷ *Delphiniums*

❸ *Corylus maxima 'Purpurea'*
(purple-leaved filbert)

❹ *Cotinus coggygria 'Notcutt's*
Variety'

❺ *Hydrangea macrophylla*
(common hydrangea)

❻ *Echinacea purpurea*
(purple coneflower)

❼ *Physostegia virginiana*
(obedient plant)

❽ *Ageratum houstonianum*
(flossflower)

Trees and shrubs

There are few blue-flowered trees and
shrubs but close together they make a
magnificent display. *Cercis siliquastrum*
(Judas tree) has clusters of rich, rose-
purple flowers on bare branches in early
summer. Markedly different is
Ceanothus × delileanus 'Gloire de Versailles',
with long spires of fragrant, powder-blue
flowers from midsummer to early fall.
And most popular of all are the blue-
flowered forms of *Hydrangea macrophylla*
(common hydrangea).

Several shrubs and trees have richly
colored leaves, including *Corylus maxima*
'Purpurea' (purple-leaved filbert), *Cotinus
coggygria* 'Notcutt's Variety' with deep-
purple leaves, and *Berberis thunbergii*
'Atropurpurea' which bears small, rich
purple-red leaves.

Climbers and wall shrubs

These provide superb displays and none
more so than California lilacs. Look for
Ceanothus impressus with clusters of deep
blue flowers in spring, and *C. thrysiflorus*

▲ *This partly cloistered water garden creates an
oasis of peace and tranquillity.*

repens with light-blue flowers. Clematis
need support and few surpass *Clematis
macropetala*, with double, light- and dark-
blue flowers in late spring and early
summer. Other blue-flowering climbers
include *Solanum crispum* (Chilean potato
vine), *Wisteria floribunda* 'Macrobotrys'
and *Abutilon vitifolium* (flowering maple).

▶ *Pale-lemon and dull-white flowers will make
the border more conspicuous in twilight.*

yellow and gold borders

These are bright and dominant, especially when in strong sunlight. Plants with these radiant colors are readily seen in the gloom of early morning and in the diminishing light of evening. Yellow is therefore useful as an edging for summer-flowering bedding displays.

Flower borders

Herbaceous borders are sometimes themed as a single color, such as yellow, but this does not mean that the border only has one color. For example, in yellow and gold borders, yellow and

◀ *Plants with narrow, yellow-variegated leaves create a dramatic shape and color constrast in a garden. Grow tender plants in pots.*

green variegated shrubs can be added to create permanency, height and contrasting color. Good yellow herbaceous perennials include *Achillea filipendulina* 'Gold Plate' (fern-leaf yarrow) with large, plate-like heads packed with deep-yellow flowers from mid- to late-summer. *Alchemilla mollis* (lady's mantle) is another superb plant, ideal for the edge of a border where it cloaks sharp, unsightly outlines.

The list of herbaceous plants for yellow borders is lengthy and includes *Coreopsis vertillata*, with bright yellow star-like flowers, dahlias, *Phlomis fruticosa* and *Verbascum bombyciferum* (mullein)— with tall flower stems and silver-haired oval leaves. Two others are *Rudbeckia fulgida* (coneflower); this has large, yellow flowers with purple-brown centers. It is superb with *Aster amellus* 'King George'. *Solidago* 'Goldenmosa' (goldenrod) bears fluffy heads of yellow flowers.

Trees and shrubs

Yellow-flowering winter and spring trees and shrubs include *Hamamelis* (witch-hazel), chimonanthus and mahonias in winter, and the glorious forsythias, *Berberis darwinii* and double-flowered gorse in spring. Many continue their display into summer, and later. Add accents of color by grouping plants in attractive duos. Around the spreading branches of *Hamamelis mollis* (Chinese witch-hazel) plant the winter-flowering *Rhododendron mucronulatum* with funnel-shaped, rose-purple flowers. For a summer leaf-color contrast, plant the deciduous shrub *Cotinus coggygria* 'Royal Purple', with dark plum-colored leaves.

BACKGROUND HARMONIES AND CONTRASTS

Yellow is a dramatic color, especially when highlighted by a contrasting background. Yellow flowers look good against a white background, while lemon-colored flowers are better suited to a red brick wall.

Climbers and wall shrubs

These range from annuals to shrubs and include the popular *Thunbergia alata*, (black-eyed Susan), a half-hardy annual raised in gentle warmth in spring before being planted in a border or against a trellis when all risk of frost has passed. Alternatively, it will scale a tripod of canes or poles. For winter color against a wall, plant *Jasminum nudiflorum*, the winter-flowering jasmine which produces bright yellow flowers on bare stems throughout winter.

Several slightly tender shrubs benefit from being planted on the sunny side of a wall and include *Cytisus battandieri*, (Pineapple broom). In midsummer it has pineapple-scented, cone-shaped, golden-yellow heads of flowers amid large, gray leaves like the laburnum. *Piptanthus nepalensis*, still better known as *Piptanthus laburnifolius* (evergreen laburnum), is also slightly tender and bears pea-shaped, bright yellow flowers like those of the laburnum in late spring and early summer. The deciduous and vigorous *Lonicera tragophylla* (Chinese woodbine)

for covering archways, pergolas, and walls. It produces bright golden-yellow flowers from early to midsummer.

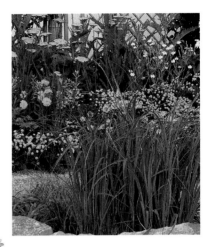

▶ *Yellow and gold borders introduce vitality into a garden, with plants ranging from yellow-leaved border plants to glorious sunflowers.*

Key to planting

❶ *Rudbeckia fulgida* (coneflower)

❷ *Euonymus fortunei* 'Emerald 'n' Gold'

❸ *Helianthus annuus* (sunflower)

❹ *Thunbergia alata* (black-eyed Susan)

❺ *Verbascum bombyciferum* (mullein)

❻ *Achillea filipenndulina* 'Gold Plate' (fern-leaf yarrow)

❼ *Solidago* 'Goldenmosa' (goldenrod)

❽ *Tagetes erecta* (African marigolds)

▲ *Gardens packed with yellow flowers and foliage are full of vitality. Hoop-like arches add interest and help to create height in a garden.*

white and silver schemes

With their brightness and purity, white flowers have a dramatic impact in strong sunlight. Silver is less dominant and is often described as grayish-white. It is less apparent because silver reflects light at many angles, whereas smooth-surfaced white petals are better reflectors of light.

Flower borders

There are many plants for gray, silver, and white herbaceous borders. Those with gray and silver foliage include *Anaphalis triplinervis* (pearly everlasting) with narrow, silver-gray, lance-shaped leaves that reveal white, wooly undersides. It also bears bunched heads of white flowers during late summer. Its near relative, *Anaphalis margaritacea yedoensis,*

◀ *Borders with white flowers and silver foliage sparkle in even the smallest amount of light, bringing unexpected vibrancy to a garden.*

has gray leaves and heads of white flowers from midsummer to fall.

Many artemisias have silver-colored leaves and none better than *Artemisia absinthium* 'Lambrook Silver', with its silvery-gray, finely divided leaves and small, round, yellow flowers during mid- and late-summer. *Artemisia ludoviciana,* the white sage, has upright stems, deeply divided, wooly white leaves, and silver-white flowers during late summer and early fall. *Onopordum acanthium* (Scotch thistle) produces broad, jagged silver-gray leaves.

The range of silver-leaved plants continues with *Stachys byzantina* (lamb's ears), with oval leaves densely covered in white, silvery hairs that create a wooly appearance. The half-hardy perennial *Senecio cineraria*, usually grown as a half-hardy annual, clothes borders with deeply lobed leaves covered in white, wooly hairs. Herbaceous plants with white flowers include the popular *Leucanthemum maximum*, still better known as *Chrysanthemum maximum* (Shasta daisy), with masses of large, white, daisy-like flowers with yellow centers from mid- to late-summer. *Gypsophila paniculata* (baby's breath) creates clouds of white flowers amid gray-green leaves. With fewer but larger white flowers, *Romneya coulteri* (California tree poppy) blooms from midsummer to fall.

The half-hardy annual *Lobularia maritima*, better known as *Alyssum maritimum* (sweet alyssum), is ideal as an edging to summer-flowering bedding arrangements.

BACKGROUND HARMONIES AND CONTRASTS

Backgrounds suitable for white flowers are limited, and they usually look their best against a red brick wall. This color also suits silver-colored foliage.

Key to planting

1 *Onopordum acanthium* (Scotch thistle)

2 *Anaphalis margaritacea yedoensis*

3 *Artemisia ludoviciana* (white sage)

4 *Carpenteria californica*

5 *Wisteria sinensis* 'Alba' (white Chinese wisteria)

6 *Romneya coulteri* (Californian tree poppy)

7 *Leucanthemum maximum* (Shasta daisy)

8 *Stachys byzantina* (lamb's ears)

Trees and shrubs

The excellent range includes *Amelanchier lamarckii* (Juneberry) with a mass of white flowers in spring, while *Eucryphia × nymansensis* produces 2¾in/6.5cm-wide, white or cream flowers in late summer and early fall. Other fine shrubs to consider are *Hydrangea arborescens* 'Grandiflora' with pure white flowers in slightly rounded heads from midsummer to early fall. Its relative *H. paniculata* 'Grandiflora' develops large, pyramidal, terminal heads of white flowers during late summer and fall.

Few small-garden shrubs with white flowers are as attractive as *Magnolia stellata* (star magnolia), with 4in/10cm-wide flowers during spring. The narrow, silver-gray, willow-like leaves of *Pyrus salicifolia* 'Pendula' are also attractive, and during spring, pure white flowers appear in terminal clusters. It is best set off by blue spring-flowering bulbs. *Spiraea × 'Arguta'* (bridal wreath) and *Viburnum opulus* 'Sterile', sometimes known as *V. o.* 'Roseum', are other superb shrubs for planting in white borders.

▲ A garden seat creates an ideal pivot for this white and silver garden, and is an ideal theme for a small garden where vibrancy is desired.

▲ Plants in pots, placed on a well-drained surface, create an attractive feature and are ideal as a focal point in small gardens.

variegated foliage

Foliage with several colors never fails to attract attention, and these qualities are found in a wide range of plants from herbaceous perennials to trees, shrubs, and climbers. Many have subdued colors, while others are bright and make a garden look vibrant.

Flower borders

There are more variegated herbaceous perennials than might, at first thought, be considered possible. Well-known variegated hostas include *Hosta fortunei albopicta*, *H. crispula* and *H.* 'Gold Standard'. There are many other hostas but perhaps one of the most unlikely variegated plants is *Aegopodium podagraria* 'Variegatum' (variegated goutweed or bishopsweed). It is not highly invasive, but is best grown in large tubs where it brightens patios with light-green leaves edged with white. The perennial grass *Hakonechloa macra* 'Aureola' is also superb in a large tub or at the corner of a raised bed. Its arching, ribbon-like leaves are variegated buff and gold, with touches of bronze.

Also ideal for borders with their vertical growth are *Iris pallida,* 'with sword-like, green and yellow striped leaves, and *I. p.* 'Argentea Variegata', with white stripes. The variegated phloxes 'Norah Leigh' and 'Harlequin' are both excellent in herbaceous borders, while *Yucca filamentosa* 'Variegata', with its sword-like leaves, always attracts attention. Give it a prominent position.

Trees and shrubs

These often create dominant displays, especially *Euonymus fortunei* 'Emerald 'n' Gold', a dense, bushy evergreen with variegated bright gold leaves; in winter they are tinged bronze-pink. 'Emerald Gaiety' and 'Silver Queen' also have variegated leaves. *Aucuba japonica* 'Variegata' is also an old garden favorite with its yellow spotted green leaves creating a dominant display. It looks good in spring when surrounded by daffodils. *Elaeagnus pungens* 'Maculata' is another evergreen favorite, with stiff, leathery green leaves splashed gold.

Salvia officinalis 'Icterina' grows about 12in/30cm high and is ideal for planting beside a path, where it cloaks unsightly edges. With its green and gold leaves it

◀ *This small, decorative, rail-type fence harmonizes with ornamental grasses and low-growing plants to create an attractive feature.*

makes an eye-catching feature. An equally striking variety is 'Tricolor', with gray-green leaves splashed creamy white, suffused with pink.

The deciduous *Cornus alba* 'Spaethii' (dogwood) has light-green leaves with irregular gold-splashed edges, with the bonus of bright red stems in winter. A near relative, *C. alternifolia* 'Argentea', is a small tree or a large shrub with horizontally spreading branches bearing small green leaves with creamy white edges. Do not hide its attractive shape.

Variegated hollies have a permanent role in gardens, adding brightness throughout the year. *Ilex × altaclerensis* 'Lawsoniana' has green leaves, usually spineless, each with a central yellow splash. It bears orange-red berries in winter. *Ilex aquifolium* has many varieties with variegated, spine-edged leaves, notably 'Golden Queen' with cream-streaked green stems and large leaves broadly edged with gold.

Climbers and wall shrubs

Perhaps the best-known variegated climbers are ivies. They range from the small-leaved *Hedera helix* 'Goldheart',

now known as 'Oro di Bogliasco', with dark green leaves splashed yellow, to large-leaved types. They include the variegated *H. canariensis* 'Gloire de Marengo' (Canary Island ivy), with deep green leaves and silver-gray and white variegations. There are several variegated forms of the Persian ivy; *H. colchica* 'Dentata Variegata' has leaves conspicuously edged creamy yellow, and 'Sulphur Heart' has irregular yellow splashes. *Actinidia kolomikta*, a deciduous climber, has green leaves that develop pink-flushed white areas toward the tips.

▶ *Trailing and spreading plants help to clothe the edges of decking. Regular trimming may be necessary to prevent them becoming intrusive.*

▼ *Variegated plants soften this flight of steps and complement the distinctive tiered branches of* Cornus controversa *('Variegata').*

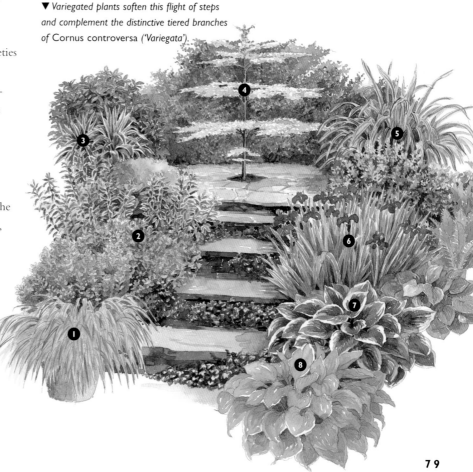

Key to planting

1. *Hakonechloa macra* 'Aureola'
2. *Phlox* 'Norah Leigh'
3. *Yucca fillamentosa* 'Variegata'
4. *Cornus alternifolia* 'Argentea'
5. *Variegated phormium*
6. *Iris pallida* 'Argentea Variegata'
7. *Hosta sieboldiana* 'Frances Williams'
8. *Hosta fortunei albopicta*

mixed color borders

There are two ways to consider "mixed" colors: one is a medley of colors within seed-raised plants such as summer-flowering bedding plants for beds and containers. The other is planning the arrangement of individual colors and this is most dramatically achieved in the larger theater of a garden.

Using mixed colors

Window boxes, wall baskets, and hanging baskets look wonderful when planted with a single species or variety in a range of colors. For example, trailing lobelia comes in white, blue, lilac, crimson, and red varieties, and all are sold together as mixed seed. A practical advantage of devoting a hanging basket to one variety in a mix of colors is that all the plants will be equally vigorous, and none will grow to dominate its neighbor.

Mixing colors

Mixing colors in a garden is as much a matter of personal preference as one of science. It is useful to use a color wheel formed of three main colors—yellow, blue, and red—and three secondaries—orange, green, and violet—to reveal those that complement or harmonize.

Complementary colors are those with no common pigments, while those that harmonize share some pigments. Yellow and violet, blue and orange, and red and green are complementary, while yellow harmonizes with green and orange, blue with green and violet, and red with orange and violet.

▲ *Plants with variegated leaves create color throughout summer and, if evergreen, the entire year. Many can be grown in pots and tubs.*

SHINY AND MATT SURFACES

The surface of a leaf influences the way it reflects light. A smooth surface reflects light at the same angle at which it is struck, and makes the light appear bright. If the surface is matt, light is reflected at different angles and creates a dull surface. In nature, however, few plant surfaces are as smooth as glass, and the scattering of light occurs from most of them.

Mixing and matching

Color planning a garden need not involve vast areas or be expensive. Consider planting a corner of a shrub border, or an area of a wall to start with.

Yellow and gold—many yellow-leaved trees and shrubs form ideal backdrops for purple-leaved plants. If the ratio of yellow to purple is about three to one they appear well-balanced. Plant the dark-leaved *Berberis thunbergii atropurpurea* with yellow-leaved shrubs like *Sambucus racemosa* 'Plumosa Aurea' (European red elder).

Key to planting

1 *Calendula officinalis* (pot marigold)

2 *Coreopsis verticillata*

3 *Cotinus coggygria* 'Notcutt's Variety'

4 *Philadelphus coronarius* 'Aureus'

5 Lupins – in mixed colors

6 *Berberis thunbergii atropurpurea*

7 *Papaver orientale* (Oriental poppy)

8 *Geranium* 'Johnson's Blue'

Blue and purple—to create a blue background display, plant *Ceanothus* 'Cascade' against a sheltered sunny wall. It grows about 10ft/3m high and wide, and bears small, rich blue flowers in late spring and early summer. For added interest, plant the slightly tender, evergreen shrub *Choisya ternata* (Mexican orange blossom) in front of it.

Red and pink—take care when using red because it is dominant, and can be overpowering. Against a mid-green background, bright-red flowers such as the hardy annual *Papaver rhoeas* (field poppy) have a three-dimensional effect. However, most red flowers are not totally color saturated and appear more as shades. Pink is a desaturated red and is easier to blend into a garden.

▲ Multicolored hanging baskets always capture attention and often suit more backgrounds than those of a single color.

▼ Packed borders with mixed colors are ideal features in small gardens. Remove dead flowers to encourage repeat flowering.

apples and pears

Apples are among the easiest tree fruit to grow in temperate climates. Pears are also popular, but they are a little harder to grow. Dessert varieties need a sunnier and more wind-sheltered position than apples. In small gardens, grow apples as cordons or espaliers.

Planting and growing apples

In the past, apple trees often grew 20ft/6m high or more, and were difficult to prune and harvest. Today, a dwarf bush apple on an M27 rootstock is ideal for a small garden, where it grows about 6ft/1.8m high and produces 12–16lb/5.4–7.2kg of fruit each year. Cordons, when grown on a similar rootstock and planted 18in/45cm apart, produce 5–7lb/2.2–3.1kg of fruit. Espaliers planted about 14ft/4.2m apart bear 20–30lb/9–13kg of fruit. Bushes demand less pruning than cordons, while espaliers need more attention.

Choose a frost-free site in full sun with shelter from strong wind. Sun is essential to ripen highly colored dessert varieties. Apples usually flower in the early part of late spring; in areas where frosts repeatedly occur at that time, select a late-flowering variety.

Well-drained moisture-retentive soil is essential, especially for dessert varieties. Cooking apple trees grow well on heavier soil. Bare-rooted trees are planted during their dormant period in winter. When planting out, mix in plenty of well-decayed garden compost or manure.

Container-grown trees can be planted whenever the soil is not frozen or waterlogged. Spring is best. Support cordons and espaliers with galvanized wires tensioned between strong posts 8–12ft/2.4–3.6m apart; space the wires 15–18in/38–45cm apart to about 7ft/2.1m high. Check the posts every spring for wind damage.

◄ *Apple trees can be grown in tubs or large pots, but plant only those growing on dwarf rootstocks.*

APPLE TREES IN TUBS

An apple tree in a container on a patio is an ideal way to grow fruit in a small garden. Dwarf rootstocks such as M27 (trees in containers grow to about 5ft/1.5m high) and M9 (up to 8ft/2.4m) make this possible, using 15in/38cm-wide wooden tubs or pots. Well-drained, moisture-retentive compost is essential and in summer regular watering is needed, sometimes every day. During winter it may be necessary to wrap straw around the tub to prevent the roots freezing and getting damaged. A plastic sheet can also be used to prevent the compost from becoming too wet. Repotting every other late winter is essential, as well as feeding during summer. Large crops are not possible but good varieties to seek include 'Gravenstein', 'Fiesta', 'Liberty' and 'Sunrise'.

Planting and growing pears

The range of rootstocks for pears is limited so that it is not possible to grow pears on trees as small as dwarf apples. Few gardens can accommodate pear trees up to 20ft/6m high, and therefore in small areas it is best to grow pears as cordons or espaliers. Cordon pears planted 18in/75cm apart each produce 4–6lb/1.8–2.7kg of fruit a year, while an espalier yields 15–25lb/6.8–11.3kg.

The same methods are used for planting and supporting pears as for apples, but pears are more susceptible to drought than apples, so be prepared to water the soil copiously during dry periods. It is probably better to select a dessert variety than a cooker, but it will need a compatible pollinator that will flower at the same time. For example, 'Conference' is partly self-fertile and needs other varieties, such as 'Seckel' or 'Harrow Delight'. Alternatively, if you have a warm garden plant the superb 'Comice', also 'Highland' (this has the bonus of keeping the fruits from late fall to early winter).

Cordon
Single, inclined stem

Espalier
Tiered branches

Espalier supports

Straining bolt   Tensioned wire

▶ *Pears grown as cordons or espaliers are best for planting in a small garden. The fruits are easily picked without using stepladders.*

peaches, nectarines, and plums

Peaches and nectarines need a warm climate. They are closely related; nectarines are smooth-skinned sports (mutations) of peaches, which have fuzzy skins. Nectarines are less hardy than peaches and have smaller yields. Plums are easily grown stone fruits.

Growing peaches and nectarines

In temperate climates, with the likelihood of frost in early and mid-spring and a general lack of pollinating insects at that time, it is often difficult to grow peaches and nectarines successfully.

Where conditions are least favorable, choose a peach rather than a nectarine, and always grow it as a fan trained on galvanized wires against a warm, sunny, south or southwest facing wall rather than as a bush.

Choose a reliable variety such as 'Harbrite' or 'Reliance'. Fortunately, peaches and nectarines are self-fertile.

Construct tiers of galvanized wires before planting a peach or nectarine. Position the lowest wire 1ft/30cm above the ground, with others 8in/20cm apart to a height of about 6ft/1.8m. Secure the wires 4in/10cm from the wall. Because peaches and nectarines are best grown against a wall it is essential to prepare the soil thoroughly by adding plenty of moisture-retentive, well-decayed garden compost or manure. Prepare an area 18in/45cm deep and 3½ft/1m square and position the main stem about 9in/23cm from the wall. Plant bare-rooted specimens in late fall or early winter, and container-grown plants at any time when the soil and weather allow. Choose a two- or three-year-old plant with eight or more branches.

Rather than tie stems directly to the wires, secure them to bamboo canes, and then to the wires. The two main arms should be at an upward 45° angle, with other stems spaced out.

▲ *Plant a fan-trained peach tree against a warm, sunny wall. To maintain the shape, secure the branches to tiers of galvanized wires.*

Always prune peaches and nectarines in late winter or early spring, when growth begins, but never tackle this task in winter. Initially, the purpose of pruning is to encourage the development of a fan. Pruning a two- or three-year-old plant is much easier than creating a fan from a rooted shoot with no side-shoots. On an established plant, cut back each arm of the fan by about one third, making cuts slightly above a downward pointing bud. In the following summer, shoots develop on each arm; allow three to form and tie each of them to a cane. Also, use a thumb to rub out buds growing toward the wall. During late summer, when each of these shoots is 18in/45cm long, nip out their growing points. Pick the fruit when the skin reveals a reddish flush and the flesh around the stalk softens—midsummer to early fall.

Growing plums

These are popular fruits. Because they flower early in the year and are vulnerable to frost, plant them in a mild, frost-free area. Dessert plums especially need a warm, sunny position to encourage good flavor. Plums can be grown in several forms, including standards, half-standards, bushes and pyramids, but in small gardens a fan-trained form is better.

Prepare the soil in the same way as for peaches and nectarines, and with a similar arrangement of tiered wires against a wall. Also, plant and prune fan-trained plants in the same way. Pick fruit from the latter part of midsummer to late fall, when it parts readily from the tree.

▼ *Plum trees flower early in the season and therefore need a warm, sheltered position against a wall. This is an ideal form for small gardens.*

Fan-trained

HAND POLLINATING

Peaches and nectarines flower early in the year when pollinating insects are scarce. Therefore, use a soft brush or loose ball of cotton wool to gently dab each flower every other day from the time the buds open until the petals fall.

growing soft fruits

It is surprising how many different types of soft fruits can be grown in a small garden. Raspberries grow vertically, while blackcurrant bushes take up only a little space. Strawberries may be grown alongside paths to be easily accessible, but if space is restricted they can be grown in a barrel.

Strawberries

There are several forms of these popular, easily grown fruits, including perpetual and alpine, but the summer-fruiting varietes are most widely grown. Once planted, they are usually left for three or four years before being discarded, with fresh beds prepared for new plants. It is possible to grow summer-fruiting types as an annual crop producing high quality fruit, but they will not grow as prolifically as well-established two- or three-year-old plants. Plant bare-rooted, summer-fruiting varieties between midsummer and early fall, and container-grown plants at any time when the soil is workable. In practice, however, they are best planted at the same time as bare-rooted plants.

Prepare strawberry beds by digging the soil in late spring or early summer, and adding well-decomposed garden compost or manure. Remove and burn perennial weeds. Just before planting, dust the surface with a general fertilizer. When planting bare-rooted plants, spread out the roots over a small mound of soil at the bottom of the hole, and check that the crown of the plant is level with the surrounding ground. Firm the soil around the roots. With container-grown plants do not bury the crown but keep it level with the soil surface. After planting, water the soil thoroughly and pull up weeds regularly.

During the following spring, sprinkle a general fertilizer around the plants, water the soil and add a mulch of straw to keep fruit off the soil. When the fruits are red all over, pick them with the calyx attached early in the morning.

Raspberries

There are two types of raspberry, summer- and fall-fruiting. Established summer-fruiting varieties produce most fruit. Both require annual pruning.

A tiered framework of wires is essential, using strong posts (up to 12ft/3.6m apart) with galvanized wires strained between them at a height of 3ft/75cm, 3½ft/1m and 5¼ft/1.6m above ground. Plant bare-rooted canes during late fall and early winter, or in early spring, spacing them 18in/45cm apart. Immediately after planting, cut all canes to 9–12in/23–30cm high just above a healthy bud.

During the first year, young canes develop and will fruit the following year. Pick the berries when fully colored yet still firm.

▲ *Blackberry 'Oregon Thornless' has medium-sized fruits in late summer and early fall and can be planted against a trellis or an arch.*

Blackcurrants

These are borne on deciduous bushes for picking during the latter part of midsummer and late summer. Position each plant slightly deeper than usual to allow for soil settlement, and encourage the development of shoots from below. Space plants 5ft/1.5m apart, and cut all stems to about 1in/2.5cm above the surface. Plant young, container-grown bushes at any time of the year when the soil and weather allow. If you plant in summer, wait until the fall and cut out all the old shoots to soil level. Prune fall to spring planting immediately.

STRAWBERRIES IN BARRELS

For more than 100 years strawberries have been grown in wooden barrels with holes cut in their sides. Good drainage is essential. Drill drainage holes in the bottom of the barrel, add clean rubble and place a 4–6in/10–15cm-wide wire-netting tube filled with drainage material in the center. Fill the barrel with well-drained compost, and put a plant into each hole.

▲ *Growing strawberries in pots is popular in small gardens. It is a good way to prevent slugs and snails damaging the fruits.*

Well-drained compost

Central core of drainage material

Drainage hole

Planting blackcurrants

Spread out roots

Cut all stems to 1in/2.5cm above the soil's surface

Planting strawberries

Bare-rooted plant

Spread out the roots over a small mound

Pot-grown plant

Rootball level with the surface

vegetables for small gardens

Some vegetables, such as asparagus and globe artichokes, are perennials, and once established continue producing crops for several years. Others are sown each year and are rotated around a vegetable plot to insure that they produce the best possible crops.

Salad crops

These are popular and easily grown; there are many interesting and colorful varieties to choose from.

✿ Outdoor cucumbers—also known as ridge cucumbers, are easily grown in fertile, moisture-retentive soil. They are best grown in a warm, sunny position sheltered from cold wind.

In mid-spring dig a hole 12in/30cm deep and wide. Fill it with a mixture of equal parts of topsoil and well-decayed garden compost or manure, and make a mound of soil on the surface. In late spring or early summer, sow three seeds ¾in/18mm deep and 2in/5cm apart. Water and cover them with a large jelly-jar. Water regularly and after germination remove the cover. Later, pull up the two weakest seedlings. When sideshoots have five or six leaves, pinch out their tips to just beyond a leaf joint. Water plants regularly, and feed them when the first fruits start to swell.

✿ Lettuces—these are popular, with a wide range of types. They include Butterheads (cabbage-type, with large, soft, smooth-edged leaves); Crispheads (another cabbage-type, with rounded heads and curled and crisp leaves); Romaine lettuces (upright growth and oblong heads); Loose-leaf lettuces (masses of loose, wavy-edged leaves that are picked individually).

◀ *Vegetables can be grown in even the smallest garden and often close together. Where possible, choose moderately vigorous varieties.*

By sowing seeds at various times, lettuces can be harvested throughout most of the year, though summer-sown lettuces are the easiest to grow. From mid-spring to the early part of late summer, sow seeds thinly and evenly in ½in/12mm-deep drills 10in/25cm apart. Keep the area moist. When seedlings are about 1in/2.5cm high, thin them first to 4in/10cm apart and later to 12in/30cm. Thin small varieties to 10in/25cm apart. From the latter part of early summer to fall harvest the lettuces.

✿ Radishes—from mid-spring to late summer, sow seeds evenly and thinly every two weeks. Form drills ½in/12mm deep and 6in/15cm apart. Germination takes five to seven days and when the seedlings are large enough to handle, thin them to 1in/2.5cm apart. Re-firm the soil around them and water it. Harvest the radishes when they are young. If left, they become woody.

✿ Scallions—in addition to bulbing types, there are scallions, also known as salad onions and bunching onions, which are delicious in salads.

TOMATOES ON A PATIO

To grow tomatoes successfully choose a sheltered, sunny position, preferably in front of a south-facing wall. On a patio tomatoes can be grown in large pots or in a growing bag. When they are grown in pots the tall stems will need to be supported with bamboo canes, but for plants in a growing bag, a proprietary supporting framework is better. Plant two tomato plants in a standard-size bag. There are two types of tomato plants: cordon and bush. Cordon types produce side-shoots which must be snapped off when the plants are young, while bush tomatoes do not require this treatment. When cordon tomatoes have produced four trusses of fruits, pinch out the shoot at two leaves above the top truss. Water and feed plants regularly throughout the summer and pick the fruit as it ripens.

Growing bag

Keep the compost moist

Water the rootball before planting

▲ *Varieties with globular roots are quick and easy to grow. Sow seeds evenly and thinly.*

▼ *Vegetable gardens can be decorative and with plenty of eye appeal. Vegetables can also be grown alongside flowers in cottage gardens.*

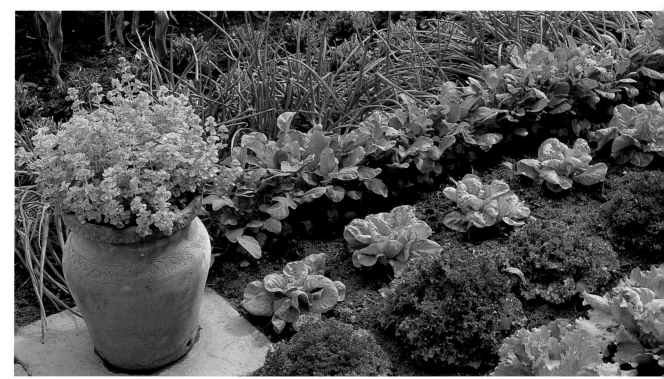

growing herbs in small gardens

Several herbs, such as the biennial angelica, are large and dominant—and best planted in herbaceous or large herb borders. Most herbs though, are suitable for small gardens, while prostrate types can be planted between paving slabs arranged in a chessboard pattern.

MAKING A HERB CARTWHEEL

Dig the soil, removing perennial weeds and, if necessary, mix in well-decayed garden compost to assist water retention. Firm the soil evenly, then rake level. Tie the ends of a 3ft/90cm-long piece of string to two canes and insert one in the center of the bed. Use the other end to scribe a circle 6ft/1.8m in diameter. Place small pebbles in a 10–12in/25–30cm-wide circle in the center, and larger pebbles around the perimeter.

Mark the positions of the spokes with more pebbles, creating 'triangles' about 15in/38cm wide at the base. Water the plants in their containers the day before planting, then arrange them in their pots in the cartwheel in an attractive design. Plant them out, water the soil and, for more intense color, cover the soil with colored gravels.

Cartwheel herb gardens

These are ornamental and functional features that can be tailored to fit areas only 6ft/1.8m square. If possible, use an old cartwheel, but a simulated design is easily created by using large pebbles to mark out the circumference and spokes.

Checkerboard designs

This is a novel way to grow low-growing herbs. Select an area, perhaps 7½ft/2.28m square, and prepare the soil as for a cartwheel garden. Then lay 18in/45cm-square paving slabs in a checkerboard arrangement leaving alternate squares uncovered. Plant the uncovered squares with a selection of low-growing herbs. Where herbs do not completely cover the soil, spread pea gravel or stone chippings over the soil. This will look attractive and has the added advantage of reducing moisture loss.

▼ *Herb wheels, closely planted with segments of contrasting thymes, create an attractive feature that is easy to manage.*

Nine popular herbs

Caraway—biennial with fern-like leaves and umbrella-like heads of green flowers.

Chives—bulbous, with tubular leaves and rose-pink flowers.

Dill—hardy annual with feathery green leaves and umbrella-like heads of yellow flowers.

Fennel—herbaceous perennial with blue-green leaves and golden-yellow flowers in large, umbrella-like heads.

Lemon balm—herbaceous perennial with lemon-scented green leaves.

Mint—herbaceous perennial with invasive roots. Wide range, from spearmint to apple mint.

Parsley—biennial, with crinkled or flat (more strongly flavored) green leaves.

Sage—short-lived shrub, with gray-green leaves and spires of violet-blue flowers in early summer. There are forms with more ornamental leaves (purple, and

some variegated) but they are mainly used to create color in borders.

Thyme—low-growing, shrubby perennial. Garden thyme is a superb culinary herb, but there are varieties with colored leaves that may be used to add color to checkerboard designs.

▼ *Enhance herb gardens by positioning small and low-growing herbs in spaces left when paving slabs are laid in a checkerboard pattern.*

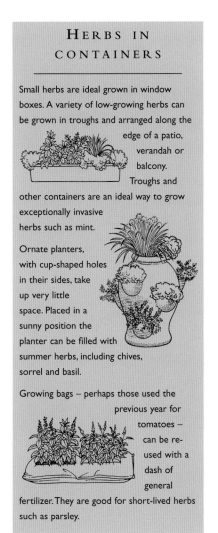

HERBS IN CONTAINERS

Small herbs are ideal grown in window boxes. A variety of low-growing herbs can be grown in troughs and arranged along the edge of a patio, verandah or balcony. Troughs and other containers are an ideal way to grow exceptionally invasive herbs such as mint.

Ornate planters, with cup-shaped holes in their sides, take up very little space. Placed in a sunny position the planter can be filled with summer herbs, including chives, sorrel and basil.

Growing bags – perhaps those used the previous year for tomatoes – can be re-used with a dash of general fertilizer. They are good for short-lived herbs such as parsley.

greenhouse gardening

Greenhouses add a dimension to gardening in a temperate climate, enabling a wider range of plants to be grown. Summer-flowering bedding plants can be sown in gentle warmth in late winter and early spring for later planting in borders and containers when all risk of frost has passed.

Range of greenhouses

Greenhouses range in shape, structure, and size, giving a very wide choice. Where possible, choose the largest greenhouse you can afford that will fit into your garden. Growing plants in greenhouses often becomes a passion demanding ever more space.

❀ Even-span—also called full-span greenhouses, have a traditional outline with a ridged sloping glass roof. Traditionally made of wood, they have a low brick or wood-paneled base, and glass above. Wooden designs are available but aluminum types are popular; these have glass from the ground to the apex.

Even-span greenhouses about 8ft/2.4m wide have a central path, and 3ft/90cm-wide areas on both sides that can be used for staging or growing plants such as tomatoes at ground level. Where a greenhouse is 6ft/1.8m or 7ft/2.1m wide, the spaces will be smaller but still thoroughly practical.

❀ Lean-to greenhouses—these are designed in width and length to suit the wall they are constructed against. Most lean-to greenhouses are glazed from soil level to the top, but with a brick surround to about 2½ft/75cm high they begin to look like a conservatory, especially where there is direct entry into the house.

❀ Hexagonal greenhouses—these have a more modern design and are becoming increasingly popular. They are usually constructed of aluminum with glass. Staging can be bought to fit.

❀ Mini greenhouses—these are for gardens with only enough room for a tiny lean-to structure, which can be

◀ *Wood-framed lean-to greenhouses are ideal for mature and informal gardens. Aluminum-framed types have a rather more clinical look.*

positioned against a garden wall, a stout fence, or the house. Proprietary staging is available and young plants can be raised in them in spring. However, because the volume of air inside is small, dramatic fluctuations in temperature can occur when the front is closed.

Wood or metal?

Greenhouses were traditionally built with a wooden frame, but increasingly aluminum is now used.

❀ Timber—the type of wood used markedly influences its longevity. Baltic red wood, also known as yellow deal, is used but needs regular painting. Western red cedar is more durable and, instead of being painted, is regularly coated in

linseed oil. The Victorians used long-lasting oak and teak, but nowadays their high cost usually makes them prohibitively expensive.

❀ Aluminum—this is widely used and, when glass is added, creates a strong structure. The extruded aluminum is designed so that both shelving and insulation brackets can be attached. Because the glazing bars are narrower than those of wood, much more light enters the greenhouse.

▶ *Aluminum-framed greenhouses are available in many interesting shapes, including a wigwam (right) and a hexagonal shape.*

▼ *The all-glass, aluminum-framed greenhouse enables the maximum amount of light to enter the structure.*

POSITIONING A GREENHOUSE

Choosing the right position in a garden for a greenhouse can reduce fuel bills. Try to:

❀ Position full-span greenhouses so that the span runs east-to-west. Position lean-to types, put them against a south- or west-facing wall.

Where possible, position doors on the side away from the prevailing wind. If the door is hinged ensure that it does not open directly into the wind; similarly, if it slides, check that it first opens on the side away from the prevailing wind.

❀ Avoid positions under overhanging trees which block out light; a snapping branch could also cause damage.

❀ Because strong winds in late winter and early spring soon cool a greenhouse, plant an evergreen hedge several yards away on the north or windward side.

index

PICTURE CREDITS

Liz Eddison/Designers: Artisan Landscape Company, Tatton Park 2000 51r/David Brum, Hampton Court 2000 74b, 206b/Chelsea 2000 37bl/Julian Dowle 27/Kevin Dunne, Tatton Park 2000/Alison Evans, Tatton Park 2000 17t/Guy Farthing, Hampton Court 2000 fcovb, 29/Alan Gardner, Hampton Court 2000 21/Carol Klein 10b, 77b/Lindsay Knight, Chelsea 2000 33/Land Art, Hampton Court 2000 16-17b, 28b/Natural & Oriental Water Garden 52/Room in the Garden 37t/Alan Sargent, Chelsea 1999 31t Chelsea 2000 12, 20b, 53/Paul Stone covflapl, 38b/Michael Upward & Richard Mercer 65/Pamela Woods, Hampton Court 1999 75. Neil Holmes 83, 86, 66b; Harry Smith Collection 51l, 84, 85; David Squire 59, 63. Illustrator: Ann Winterbottom.